DO THE RIGHT THINGS!

A practical guide to ethical living

Pushpinder Khaneka

Do The Right Things!
A practical guide to ethical living

First published in the UK by
New Internationalist Publications Ltd
Oxford OX4 1BW, England
www.newint.org
New Internationalist is a registered trademark

Main cover photo by Phil Ashley
Other photos (from left to right):
Children's game, Phanthiet, Vietnam by Tran Cao Bao Long/UNEP/Still
Pineapple farmer, Ghana by Ron Giling/Still
Wind power, Belgium by Olivia Droeshaut/Still

Cartoons by Brick http://brickbats.co.uk

Design by Andrew Kokotka.

Printed on recycled paper by TJ International, Padstow, Cornwall,
England.

British Library Cataloguing in Publication Data.
A catalogue record for this book is available from the British Library.

ISBN 1 904456 17 0

DO THE RIGHT THINGS!

A practical guide to ethical living

Pushpinder Khaneka

About the author

Pushpinder Khaneka is a journalist who has worked in Britain and abroad for, among others, *The Guardian*, *The Observer* and *The Independent*. Until recently he was the deputy editor of the *Guardian Weekly*.

Send us your suggestions!

From time to time we plan to publish updated editions of *Do The Right Things!*

If you have tips, ideas and recommendations that are not included in this edition and which you think would help others whose aim is to live a greener, more ethical lifestyle, please send them to us.

We welcome your submissions by email on: dotherightthings@newint.org

Foreword
by Benjamin Zephaniah

Until now, being in public life and caring about humankind and the world around us has been very frustrating. I keep meeting all these people that care about things: some come up to me with tears in their eyes, they want to do something, they want to help, but they feel helpless and they just don't know where to go.

In supermarkets, in airports, in chemists and at reggae concerts, they keep confronting me and asking me what they can do to help, and every time this happens I am speechless. Of course I know that there are many ways to help but for some strange reason I can never remember that car-sharing club website, or Oxfam's address, or Amnesty's phone number. It's so frustrating.

I know mobile phones are dangerous, and that there's a company which will recycle them but I can never remember their name. Now things have changed. Now I can proudly tell everyone about a book called *Do The Right Things!* by a bloke called Pushpinder Khaneka. Nice bloke, good book. I even feel that I'm doing a good deed by recommending it. Indeed I can tell them that this book really is the first of its kind and that it covers topics like buying, selling, sharing and even investing. I can tell them that this is a superbly fresh and original book that comes from a place called compassion – and that was written with love.

But all that won't really matter. What will matter is that it's a practical book, an easy-to-use no-nonsense book that knows why it exists and does not strive to make you feel guilty.

This book inspires me. But let me be frank: many books have inspired me. This one, however, inspires me in a unique way. The author is not simply telling me that there is something wrong, he's telling me what I can do about it, and for most things he's giving me more than one option.

We have to keep the pressure on. We simply cannot wait for politicians to wake up and smell the pollution, we cannot wait until capitalism eats itself – individuals must take action now.

So here it is. This easy-to-read guide to becoming a better world citizen is a direct-action handbook that shows you can easily reduce your impact on the environment. The seas will rise, the rivers will flood, the air shall be heavy, darkness and famine shall be upon the land, and a man in a suit will genetically modify you – if you let him.

Don't. Power to the peaceful.

Benjamin Zephaniah

Contents

Introduction

Better to light a candle than to curse the darkness
Chinese proverb

Almost half the world's population – 2.7 billion people – lives on less than two dollars a day. And for every dollar the West gives in aid to developing countries, it takes back two through unfair trade. As globalization spreads, so does the increasing awareness that millions of people are trapped in poverty by powerful and unjust economic forces.

Pollution and global warming threaten catastrophic climate change and ecological damage. Rich countries, with only 15 per cent of the world's population, contribute disproportionately to global warming – generating 50 per cent of carbon dioxide emissions and using 50 per cent of the world's energy. The vast majority of victims of climate change (hurricanes, flooding, drought) are, and will continue to be, in developing countries.

With all that going on, it's pretty clear that the planet needs saving – and you could be one of the people to help do that. Don't just say you care, show you care.

Martin Luther King once said that: 'Before you finish eating breakfast this morning, you've depended on more than half the world.' So wake up and smell the fair trade coffee. The way you spend your money and the way you live your life can change people's lives in the developing world.

Individuals can effect real change through their everyday actions. You can do something positive for the planet by, for example, changing your shopping list, your credit card, the light bulbs in your home or recycling your rubbish.

And, as the proverb says, 'if you think you're too small to make a difference, you haven't been in bed with a mosquito'. In any case, in wanting to save the world you won't be on your own. There are already millions of people out there campaigning, protesting, donating money, volunteering and recycling – striving to make the world a better place.

Think about it...

Sometimes using a different word can make you think differently. The term 'Third World' or *tiers monde* was first used in 1952 by French demographer Alfred Sauvy, along with 'First World' (North America, Europe and Australasia) and Second World (the old Soviet Union and the 'Eastern bloc'). The last two are now little used, and 'Third World' too has become rather old hat, replaced by a variety of terms such as 'developing world', or sometimes 'the South' (as opposed to the North or the West for the rich world) or even the more accurate but less common 'Majority World'. Best probably to avoid lumping countries together in this way, though sometimes it is unavoidable. Just think before you trot out the first one that comes into your head!

Some people think that doing good is hard, and therefore best done by others. But the truth is that you don't have to make extreme life changes to make a difference. This book could have been called Easy Ways To Save The World, because none of the actions suggested call for great sacrifice. By merely tweaking your lifestyle you can do a little to help change a lot.

This book highlights the path to easy virtue. But it's much more than just a lazy person's guide to saving the world. It provides a great deal of practical information to help you make choices that make a difference.

Guides to 'good' living generally concentrate on ethical consumption and investment. *Do The Right Things!* is a more comprehensive and ambitious attempt to generate a wide range of robust responses to right the planet's wrongs. It'll help you to kick-start your campaign to do good – and to feel good about doing it.

It's your world: do something to make it better.

Listen up

'Once there was a great forest fire, and all the birds and animals rushed to escape. Humming Bird went to the river and collected a drop of water. The other birds laughed. "What are you doing?" they asked. She replied, "I'm doing what I can"'

Native American story

Consuming passions

Most people leave their consciences at home when they go shopping. But as concerns grow about social justice, the rush for profits without principles and environmental degradation, morality has entered the market. Consumers are increasingly asking questions about the working conditions of the people who make the products they buy and the true cost of goods.

As globalization spreads, many of the products in the West now come from Third World countries. Western shoppers depend on their cheap labour and natural resources. Research shows that if Africa, Asia and Latin America were to increase their share of exports by just one per cent, the gain in income would lift 128 million people out of poverty.

So you'd think the West would welcome this boost in trade and the attendant benefits. Not so. The rules of international trade are rigged in favour of the rich. Developing countries face restrictive tariff barriers for access to Western markets. At the same time, rich countries spend about $1 billion a day on agricultural subsidies to their farmers. Their products are then dumped on world markets, depressing prices and under-mining the livelihoods of millions of small farmers in poor countries. The United Nations estimates countries in the South are denied $700 billion annually because of unfair trade rules. That's a staggering amount of injustice.

Your shopping affects people in developing countries, and ethical consumption is a way to take a stand for trade justice. It's easy – all you have to do is choose one product over another. Your wallet can be a powerful weapon in the fight to put people before profits. And battle has already been joined. The Co-operative Bank's annual survey tracking ethical spending found that in 2002 more than half of shoppers switched brands or boycotted at least one product for ethical reasons. Companies lost £2.6 billion because consumers were unhappy with their behaviour. Total sales of ethical goods and services reached £6.9 billion. That sum is bound to grow as awareness among shoppers increases. And the sky's the limit, because the total market share of ethical goods and services is still less than two per cent.

So, now that you know you're far from being alone out there, you can get stuck into changing the world with your shop-ping trolley. Join the growing number of consumers calling on multinational corporations to be more responsible – be it through better working conditions for employees, greater care for the environment or severing links with repressive regimes. Bless the good companies, blame the bad and boycott the ugly – and make sure they get the message. Let companies know why you are unhappy, so that they can remedy what they're doing wrong.

Think globally, act locally may be an old cliché, but that's no reason not to put it into practice. Consumers are not powerless against corporate giants. In well-organized campaigns, they have changed corporate behaviour. Just ask the firms on the receiving end, such as McDonalds, Nike and Shell. A simple shopping choice can help to change things, and every time you buy something you can make a difference. Do as much as you can as soon as you can – and feel the warm glow of your halo.

The Trade Justice Movement is made up of a number of organizations that campaign for international trade rules to be changed to benefit the poor and the environment. Its website has good briefings and campaigning information.

Trade Justice Movement
Tel: 01865 245678
www.tradejustice.org

Oxfam has a website that highlights some of the glaring trade inequalities, provides information and encourages you to take action. It's worth a visit, even if you just buy the T-shirt!

Make Trade Fair
www.maketradefair.com

The Ethical Consumer Research Association, which publishes *Ethical Consumer* magazine, keeps tabs on developments, and signals concerns for consumers with a conscience.

Ethical Consumer
Tel: 0161 226 2929
www.ethicalconsumer.org

Be fair

Choosing to buy fair trade goods offers a real, practical option to strike a blow against the corporate empires. Fair trade bucks the so-called free market system in an attempt to redress the current iniquities. Consumers pay a guaranteed price, including a small social premium, to groups of small producers in Asia, Africa and Latin America to help them survive in a global trading system where the odds are stacked against them. It ensures decent working conditions and a long-term link-up between buyer and seller through which small farmers can plan for the future. The price of the commodity remains the same despite the volatility in world markets. It could mean that a family in Botswana or Guatemala has money to send a child to school, or that a community can open a health centre or dig a well. The consumer pays about a penny extra for a cup of coffee or a few pence extra for a banana. Which shows that salving your conscience can, sometimes, come remarkably cheap.

The Fairtrade Foundation labels goods with its 'Fairtrade' mark, which appears on more than 100 products, includ-

ing coffee, tea, bananas, chocolate, cocoa, sugar, honey and orange juice. And you can rest assured that switching to fair trade doesn't mean turning off your taste buds – there is no compromise on quality.

Sales of fair trade products in Britain reached £92 million in 2003, according to the Fairtrade Foundation, up 50 per cent on the previous year. As a result of these sales, more than 500,000 farmers and workers in the South benefit from the better deal that fair trade guarantees. But that £92 million is tiny when compared with the annual food sales figure of £100 billion – so there's still a lot of catching up to do.

Fair trade products are available at supermarkets as well as at wholefood and Oxfam shops. The Co-op is particularly good, having switched all of its own-label coffee and chocolates to fair trade. You can also buy fair trade goods by mail order from a number of suppliers, including Traidcraft.

If your local supermarket and shops don't sell fair trade goods, ask for them to be stocked. Your demands will increase the availability of the products. Also ask for fair trade goods in restaurants and cafés to raise awareness and increase their consumption.

Did you know...?

Of the world's 100 largest economies, the majority (51) are not countries but corporations. The world's top 200 corporations account for over a quarter of economic activity on the globe while employing less than one per cent of its workforce.

And you can lobby your local council to declare your borough – or even your town – a fair trade area that actively promotes fair trade goods. Contact the Fairtrade Foundation or look up its website to see what action you can take to spread the word. Meanwhile, don't hold back on acquiring a feast of fair trade goodies.

The Fairtrade Foundation
Tel: 020 7405 5942
www.fairtrade.org.uk

Traidcraft
Tel: 0870 443 1017
www.traidcraftshop.co.uk

Coffee and tea

In 2001, the price of coffee – the world's second-largest traded commodity after oil – was about 80 per cent less than it was in 1997. Although there has been a slight recovery since then, it's still barely enough for the 25 million coffee growers around the world to survive. But you don't see the price of a cappuccino on your high street coming down, as the large firms like Nestlé, Kraft and Sara Lee (which roast the coffee) pocket ever-greater profits. So while trendy coffee bars can charge almost £2 for a cappuccino, a poor coffee farmer in Central America can receive as little as a few pence. Pardon the pun, but now there's a chance to give the roasters a bit of a roasting by buying fair trade coffee. Fair trade brands such as Cafédirect have succeeded in persuading buyers to stir some human rights into their coffee. As one campaigner put it: 'Coffee brewed without the bitterness of injustice tastes better.' However, so far only about one per cent of coffee is bought under fair trade rules.

The price of tea has also dropped – in real terms – by almost half since the 1970s. Here, too, fair trade firms have stepped into the market.

Fair trade coffee and tea taste good, make you feel good and do good. Coffee and tea drinkers can make a real difference to the lives of growers. So buy fair trade and get a real kick out of your cuppa.

Make sure you drink fair trade coffee and tea at home and at work. Ask for them in supermarkets, cafés, bars, restaurants, and anywhere else you're likely to stop for a drink. Spread the word. Tell your friends. Look up the Fairtrade Foundation's and Cafédirect's websites to bone up on arguments and melt any resistance to switching to an ethical brew. The main teas are Teadirect, Clipper and Equal Exchange. The main coffee brands are Cafédirect, Equal Exchange and Percol. Union Coffee Roasters also has a superb range of single-estate, fairtrade coffees. For coffee with 'taste, passion and ethics', join the Union.

Cafédirect
Tel: 020 7490 9520
www.cafedirect.co.uk

Equal Exchange
Tel: 0131 220 3484
www.equalexchange.co.uk

Clipper
Tel: 01308 863344
www.clipper-teas.com

Union Coffee Roasters
Tel: 020 7474 8990
www.unionroasters.com

Bananas

Britain's favourite fruit has had a troubled history of exploitation and conflict. Through the years we've seen the infamous banana republics in Latin America, which multinational companies ran as virtual fiefdoms; harsh working conditions and battles for unionization; small growers squeezed out of the market by the big bad guys; and the European Union and the US squaring up over tariffs and access to the European market. And the struggles aren't over yet.

Fair trade bananas offer hope and a future to small producers. And consumer pressure has brought better conditions in some of the 'dollar brand' banana zones. Buy fair trade bananas where possible, followed by eastern Caribbean bananas, which helps small growers. Among the large companies, the best buys are Fyffes and Geest. If possible, avoid the anti-union dollar brands: Del Monte, Dole and particularly Chiquita.

Banana Link aims to help banana producers and to mobilize the public to take action. It has information about fair trade bananas and suppliers.

Banana Link
Tel: 01603 765670
www.bananalink.org.uk

Clothes

One of the most glaring examples of global trade injustice is that the US pays a $4 billion subsidy to its cotton farmers. This has driven down prices on the world market, putting more efficient African cotton farmers out of business. The Oxfam website – **www.maketradefair.com** – helpfully allows you to email George Bush to let him know what you think about this scandalous handout. So go ahead and tell him!

Cotton cultivation accounts for about 25 per cent of the world's insecticides and more than 10 per cent of its pesticides. That's

Listen up

'An ethical approach to life does not forbid having fun or enjoying food and wine, but it changes our sense of priorities'

Peter Singer (1946-), Australian philosopher and ethicist

an awful lot of poison to pour into the soil. On top of that, many of the harmful chemicals used by cotton farmers in the South are banned in the North.

And that's just at the start of the chain in the murky world of making clothes. The industry is tainted by sweatshop conditions and rights abuses. So far, not a single brand of clothing carries the Fairtrade label.

Things are changing – slowly. Some of the large clothing firms have been embarrassed by consumers into improving working conditions. A more promising development has been the growth of organic and fair trade producers. Word has it that fair trade fashion is on its way to becoming cool. But small-scale production, organic cotton at fair prices, fair wages and decent working conditions all push up costs, so the clothes aren't cheap (or, thankfully, nasty). Hopefully, as market share increases, prices will become more competitive.

When you buy clothes, don't just think aesthetics, think ethics too. In shops, ask about the firm's policy on labour standards, and how and where the clothes were made. You can also write to the bosses of your favorite brands to ask about work conditions at their factories, saying you'd love their clothes even more if ethics were woven into the fabric.

People Tree sells fashionable, organic, fair trade clothes.
Tel: 0845 450 4595
Or 020 7739 0660
www.ptree.co.uk

Natural Collection sells a range of organic cotton clothing and bed-linen.
Tel: 0870 331 3333
www.naturalcollection.com

Here are two campaigning organizations that keep tabs on developments in the industry:

Labour Behind the Label brings together pressure groups and individuals to campaign in support of garment workers.

Tel: 01603 610993
www.labourbehindthelabel.org

No Sweat is an activist organization that fights against sweatshop conditions worldwide.

Tel: 07904 431959
www.nosweat.org.uk

Chocolate

Over the past 10 years, the price of a bar of chocolate has risen by two-thirds, while the price of cocoa has dropped by about half. Who do you think has made a fat profit out of the difference? Answers on a postcard please. However, Britain being a nation of chocoholics, we're in a good position to exact sweet revenge on greedy multinationals. Make sure you only buy fair trade chocolate. The Christmas and birthday presents you give will taste even sweeter. Fair trade chocolates taste as good as any other, and they don't weigh on your conscience (even if they might do elsewhere). All the Co-op's own-brand chocolate is now fair trade. Fair trade Divine, Dubble and Green & Black's can be bought in supermarkets and Oxfam shops. And Traidcraft sells a range of chocolate goodies.

Traidcraft
Tel: 0870 443 1017
www.traidcraftshop.co.uk

Divine

www.divinechocolate.com
Dubble
www.dubble.co.uk

Green & Black's
www.greenandblacks.com

Sugar

The cost of producing sugar from beet is roughly double that of producing it from cane. Yet in pound per hectare terms sugar beet is Britain's most profitable arable crop by far. Why? Because subsidies, quotas and high tariffs on imports mean big sugar businesses in rich countries receive around 1.75 times what they would on the free market. Tropical countries which produce sugar from cane are hit with a double whammy: it's tough for them to export to rich countries, plus the prices they can earn on the world market are kept at rock bottom thanks to the huge amounts dumped on to it by cosseted sugar-beet farmers from the European Union. A suitable case for making sure you buy fair traded (cane) sugar, which has recently become available in supermarkets, as well as from online fair traders such as Traidcraft.

Traidcraft
www.traidcraftshop.co.uk

Alcohol

Co-op stores and Traidcraft sell fairly traded 'wines with a conscience' from Chile and South Africa. As the Co-op puts it: 'We trample the grapes, not the growers.'

Beer drinkers should know about the Workers Beer Company,

which is owned by trade unions and raises funds for unions and campaigning organizations. It runs beer tents at festivals. If you're putting on a large event or want to earn money for your organization by providing volunteer workers at the beer tents, get in touch. By a happy coincidence, its headquarters is also an award-winning pub – where they'd love to see you.

The Workers Beer Company
68 Clapham Manor Street
London SW4 6DZ
Tel: 020 7720 0140
www.workersbeer.co.uk

Trade fairs

Fair trade fairs, which take place in December, are the perfect place to buy your Christmas presents every year. They feature stalls run by ethical traders and campaign groups. And while we're on Christmas, all the cards you send should be charity ones, bought direct.

World Fair
Tel: 020 7354 4231
www.worldfair.org.uk

Fair Trade Fair
http://fairtradefair.com

Flower power

Charity Flowers Direct is an online flower shop owned by the charity Age Concern. Not only does it benefit from any profits, but you can choose for it to donate 15 per cent of the price of your purchase to a charity of your choice. So, to make your flowers smell twice as nice, you could, for example, ask for a slice of your gift to go to Womankind Worldwide, which supports women's development and their rights across the world.

Charity Flowers Direct
Tel: 0870 530 0600
www.charityflowers.co.uk

Womankind Worldwide
Tel: 020 7549 5700
www.womankind.org.uk

Organic growth

Sales of organic food in Britain topped £1 billion for the first time at the end of 2003, according to the Soil Association, the biggest promoter of organic food in the country. And organic shoppers appeared to be turning away from supermarkets towards local businesses. About 10 per cent of sales were at farmers' markets, farm shops and through direct delivery.

Organic farming means less use of additives, chemical fertilizers and pesticides, making it good for consumers and for the soil. Animal welfare is better, too, and they are reared without the routine use of drugs.

But there's still a long way to go for organics to enter the

mainstream. That feted £1 billion is a very small percentage of the total food market. And just 7 per cent of buyers bought about 60 per cent of the organic food on sale. So, if you didn't buy your fair share, better get cracking. If you're an organic virgin, so to speak, you can begin by buying a couple of products on a regular basis. If all goes well (and there's no reason it shouldn't) you can build on that.

You can buy organic food at your local supermarket. But even better would be to look up the Organic Directory on the Soil Association's website and check out whether there's a local outlet and any local produce in your area. The directory lists hundreds of outlets across the country as well as 'box schemes', which deliver a mixed box of produce to a central drop-off point or straight to your door. You can also find out about farmers' markets. If you can buy straight from producers, so much the better.

Don't just buy organic, choose organic options in restaurants – and if there aren't any on the menu, suggest that maybe there should be.

As consumption of organics increases, economies of scale will come into play, prices will drop, and the benefits can be enjoyed by more and more people. This will create a virtuous circle (or a merry-go-round).

The Soil Association
Tel: 0117 314 5000
www.soilassociation.org

The National Association of Farmers' Markets has a list of markets across the country, including in cities.
Tel: 0845 230 2150
www.farmersmarkets.net

Simply Organic is one of the largest home delivery firms. It delivers more than 2,000 organic products nationwide, including fruit, vegetables, meat and dairy products.

Tel: 0131 448 0440
www.simplyorganic.co.uk

Local call

If you want your local shops to survive in the face of the onslaught by the giants, make sure you use them. Much of your money will go straight back into your community and help it to prosper, rather than being siphoned off to somewhere far away. So shake off your chains where possible (ie McDonalds, Starbucks, GAP) and give your custom to local traders. Also avoid supermarkets when you can, and help to free producers and consumers from their stranglehold. As supermarkets spread their reach, their bulk-buying power sends competitors to the wall; and their squeeze on suppliers to cut prices puts a squeeze, ultimately, on Third World wages.

Find out about local produce and local markets, and you could save the planet a great deal of the polluting travel that comes from delivering goods miles away from where they are produced. For ethical consumers, it's not just what you buy, but also where you buy it.

No way

Boycotts have a long and honourable history. As early as the 18th century some Europeans boycotted sugar from the Caribbean because it was produced using slave labour. In more modern times, boycotts have been used to support migrant farmworkers in the US; to put pressure on companies trading with apartheid

South Africa; to improve conditions in sweatshops; and to back workers in banana plantations. Refusing to buy a company's products sends a message in no uncertain terms and hits them where it hurts most, right between their profits.

Do boycott campaigns really work? Yes, if enough people join in, they are well targeted, the message is clear and they are backed by people who are directly affected by the action. Megaphone diplomacy has its place. So rather than being a lone voice, link up with or organize consumer campaigns. Let companies know why you're unhappy with their behaviour and what you'd like them to do about it. Boycotts have forced multinationals to change packaging policies (McDonalds), recognize irresponsible marketing (Nestlé) and improve conditions in factories (Nike).

The Ethical Consumer website has a list of the latest boycotts.
www.ethicalconsumer.org

Co-op America runs an informative boycott site
www.boycotts.org

On some websites you can email protests and sign online petitions, so you can take to the streets (metaphorically speaking, that is) without ever leaving home.

Here are a few of the boycotts now in train:

Nestlé is the target of an international boycott in protest at its irresponsible marketing of baby milk formula as a substitute for breast milk. The World Health Organization estimates that 1.5 million infants die around the world every year because they are not breastfed. Where water is unsafe a bottle-fed child is up to 25 times more likely to die as a result of diarrhoea than a breastfed child.

The international boycott – co-ordinated by the International Baby Food Action Network – primarily targets Nescafé, the corporation's flagship product, but people are also encouraged to boycott all Nestlé products (and watch out for the well-known names that Nestlé has taken over such as Branston, Buitoni, Crosse & Blackwell, Perrier, Rowntree's, Sarsons and Ski). There are plenty of alternatives to Nestlé cereals and chocolate bars. If you're stranded with children in high summer there is sometimes only Nestlé ice cream on offer – but a Walls alternative can usually be found somewhere round the corner. Besides, children are generally very responsive to the idea of the Nestlé boycott and the link it makes between them and children in poorer countries.

So take a break from Kit Kat (one Nestlé product among many) and sign on.

Contact **Baby Milk Action**
Tel: 01223 464420
www.babymilkaction.org

Killercoke is a campaign to stop the murder and intimidation of union leaders and organizers at Coca-Cola bottling plants in Colombia.

www.killercoke.org

Also see **Cokewatch**, a website designed to keep an eye on the giant Coca-Cola company.

www.cokewatch.org

The **Stop Esso** boycott has been instigated because the company has done more than any other to scupper international action on climate change.

www.stopesso.org

Bacardi has been targeted because of its ongoing role in the US blockade of Cuba, which prevents the sale of food, medicines and other essential supplies to the country.

Rock Around the Blockade
Tel: 020 7837 1688
www.ratb.org.uk

Well travelled

Tourism is the world's biggest business. And while it can be a force for good, promoting a meeting of cultures and providing employment in poor countries, it can also be an immensely destructive force – on people and the planet. Tourism Concern has pioneered the concept of ethical tourism, raising our awareness of the effect holidays can have on communities, economies and the environment.

Most of us love cheap flights, and with good reason. But flights generate greenhouse gas emissions that contribute to climate change. Right now only about 3.5 per cent of Britain's emissions come from flights, but the rapid growth in flying (helped by those cheap prices) means that aviation's emissions are headed skywards (excuse the pun). Flights will contribute 75 per cent of emissions by 2050. No doubt, even as you read this, scientists are poring over their notes and formulas to find more fuel-efficient technologies. But before they kick in (the technologies, not the scientists), you can do something to make a difference – and I don't mean stay home and watch TV.

It is certainly true that air travel is sometimes the only means of transport to a holiday destination. But for trips closer to home, consider alternative forms of transport. For example, train travel is often the best way to see Europe and is a far more environmentally friendly way of getting around.

Savvy travellers to date have been using a scheme whereby you can 'neutralize' the global warming from your flights by planting trees to reabsorb the carbon dioxide emitted. Some companies offer the consumer the possibility to plant trees as a way to 'offset' the carbon emissions generated from plane travel and other means.

While this may sound appealing, the whole practice of offsetting emissions is heavily contested and increasingly controversial. The basic problem of overconsumption needs to be addressed. We all have a responsibility to reduce.

Instead of buying such offset products, consider giving a small donation to a local transport group or environmental advocacy organization. Your money will be far better spent.

"SURE I'D LIKE ANOTHER SHOT AT A LUNAR LANDING, GENERAL... JUST DON'T HAVE THE ACREAGE..."

Another action the thoughtful tourist can take is to avoid most package holidays. More than half of holidays abroad taken by Britons annually are part of a package deal. Yet often as little as 20 per cent of the money spent by these tourists stays in the country they visit. The rest is pocketed by tour operators here. And mass tourism can damage local communities and the environment by being responsible for – among other things – the destruction of ecosystems, water shortages and prostitution. Ethical tourism seeks to redress this balance by ensuring local people get a fair share of the revenue generated from tourism and by raising awareness of the local culture and environment. Travelling independently or with companies that spend your money locally is a step in the right direction. As is eco-tourism, which seeks to minimize the environmental impact of visitors.

So book your holiday through an ethical tour operator; avoid package and all-inclusive holidays (which exclude the locals); respect local cultures and the environment (just as you would do at home); and take your custom to local cafés and restaurants (where you can meet local people rather than fellow tourists). Oh, and another good tip: 'Haggle with humour, and remember how wealthy you are compared with the people you buy from.'

Tourism Concern publishes *The Good Alternative Travel Guide* (£9.99), which offers a wealth of information on 'good' holidays. A directory lists ethical tour operators and organizations. As the book says: 'The holidays featured here are better for you... better for the people you visit... better for the environment.' And you can't say better than that! So get clued up before paradise is truly lost.

Tourism Concern
Tel: 020 7133 3330
www.tourismconcern.org.uk

The Travel Foundation is a charity that supports sustainable tourism and aims to help visitors make a positive contribution to holiday destinations.

Tel: 0117 927 3049
www.thetravelfoundation.org.uk

North South Travel is an agency with a difference. It offers discounted fares worldwide and other travel agent services, but its profits go towards supporting projects in developing countries through its charitable trust.

Tel: 01245 608291
www.northsouthtravel.co.uk

Final good buys

Get Ethical is a large and impressive website set up by *Red Pepper* and *The Big Issue* magazines to promote ethical consumerism and support social enterprises. Apart from ethical shopping, it has links and information on social justice and environmental issues – and lots of other good stuff. It's a must-visit site!

www.getethical.org

See also **Ethical Junction**, a one-stop shop for ethical organizations and ethical trading.

www.ethicaljunction.org

If you want to be good with your gifts as well, try the *Good Gifts Guide*. Set up in 2003 by the Charities Advisory Trust, it is a catalogue packed with ideas for presents you can give your nearest and dearest. Only these are presents that go a little further: things like giving a cow to a family in India, or 'giving a braincell' – funding development of treatments for diseases like Alzheimer's, Parkinson's, meningitis and cancer – or a 'new

leash of life' to train homeless dogs; these are gifts for those who need them that make you feel great too!
www.goodgifts.org/goodgifts

And finally, there's a book you should take with you every time you go in for retail therapy. *The Good Shopping Guide*, published by the Ethical Consumer Research Association, is a comprehensive tome that points out the good guys and the bad guys among producers. Urging you to appreciate the power of your till receipt, it covers everything from boilers and baby food through to washing machines and yoghurts.

www.thegoodshoppingguide.co.uk

Easy does it

Pay close attention to what's in your shopping basket

Switch all your coffee and chocolates to fair trade

Avoid package holidays unless they are with ethical travel companies

Giving till it hurts...

Money matters

Giving money to charity can be a rewarding experience all round. It makes you feel good, and your money does good. So don't just let your money talk, make it sing. And there's probably nowhere that it'll sing sweeter than in the coffers of a charity as it lies poised to do good. Money can't buy love, as the song says, but it can certainly help to bring about social change. And no matter who you are, or how much money you have, you can do your bit to bring about that change.

Many good works depend on members of the public reaching into their pockets and coming up with the money needed. But British citizens apparently aren't as keen to give as their US counterparts. On average, the British public gives 0.5 per cent of annual income to charity, compared with 2 per cent in the US.

Research also shows that Britons are given to making spontaneous donations. Tin-rattling collections and raffle tickets take their fancy. According to the National Council for Voluntary Organizations, almost a quarter of charity donors give via street collection – more than by any other method. Yet this accounts for just three per cent of the £6.5 billion raised by charities annually.

The Government wants us to give more to good causes. And to shake much more than the loose change from our pockets, it has introduced big tax concessions. So, by making the right moves, you (and your chosen charity) can get more for your money.

Since 2000, giving money to charity has become a lot easier – and cheaper. Tax benefits given to charities and donors under

Did you know...?

British national income per person went up from $18,700 in 1995 to $25,250 in 2002, an increase of 35 per cent. Over the same period national income per person in sub-Saharan Africa went down from $501 to $460 – a decrease of 9 per cent.

the Gift Aid scheme could generate extra revenue of up to £400 million annually for good causes over the next few years.

So far, however, despite these changes, only seven per cent of donations are made in a tax-efficient way. The Government-backed Giving Campaign, which promotes tax-efficient giving, plans to boost this figure to at least 50 per cent. That would mean a lot more money for charities as well as savings for donors. According to the Giving Campaign, if everybody in the UK who gave to charity in 2002 had done so by tax-efficient means, charities would have received an extra £878 million. So givers (that means you) need to get their act together.

To encourage us to give generously, the tax rules have been simplified so that giving can be more flexible and more effective. The Charities Aid Foundation (CAF), a non-governmental organization that works with charities and their supporters, says, 'There's never been a better time to give'. You'd better believe it.

Under the Gift Aid scheme, a charity can claim back the basic rate of tax from the Inland Revenue on every donation it receives – that adds an extra 28 per cent to receipts. And if the donor is a higher-rate taxpayer, he or she can claim tax back of 18 per cent (the difference between basic rate and higher rate tax) of the total

Listen up

'Riches are like muck, which stink in a heap, but spread abroad make the earth fruitful'

an anonymous saying which may derive from something said by the English philosopher-scientist Francis Bacon (1561-1626): 'Money is like muck, not good except it be spread'.

value of the donation received by the charity. There is very little paperwork involved: donors only need to confirm that they are UK taxpayers. This can be done in writing or verbally.

So, for every £100 you give to a charity, it receives £128. And if you are a higher rate taxpayer, the donation could cost you just £77. Claiming the tax back is easy. You add up the Gift Aid donations made in the tax year and enter the total amount in your Annual Return form for the Inland Revenue.

Before you pop the champagne corks on the fact that a charity can receive a healthy whack more than you actually donated, you ought to know that there's an even better way of giving.

In this case, charity begins at the office. Under the Payroll Giving scheme, you make a regular monthly donation from your gross salary (ie before tax has been deducted). Payroll Giving can carry a triple whammy of benefits: it costs the donor a lot less, the charity has a regular source of income, and often employers match the employee's donation. For an employee giving £10 a month, it would cost a basic rate (22 per cent) taxpayer £7.80, and a higher rate (40 per cent) taxpayer only £6.

Hundreds of companies have signed up to the scheme (make sure yours has), which charities are hoping will become the bedrock of their funding. Firms with fewer than 500 employees can get grants to help set up Payroll Giving. The scheme, which beats the pants off any other system of donation, raised £86 million for charities in 2003.

The Giving Campaign
Tel: 020 7930 3154
www.givingcampaign.org.uk

The **All About Giving** website has a wealth of information on tax-effective giving.

www.allaboutgiving.org

The Charities Aid Foundation
Tel: 01732 520050
www.cafonline.com

Corporate giving

Charity may begin at home, but there's no reason it should end there. Companies are also entitled to tax concessions when giving money to charity. The donation is charged against gross income, reducing the corporation tax liability. Companies, like individuals, can open Charities Aid Foundation charity accounts (see below), which enables payments to be made to charities at any time. All payments into the account are considered charitable donations at the point of receipt, so your budget can be rolled over into the next accounting period. Ask the company you work for to set up a charity budget, highlighting the tax and other benefits. Some companies, for example, match pound for pound the money donated by their employees.

The All About Giving website (see above) has more information on what your company and staff can do for charities.

Giving shares and property

Aside from giving money, you can gift listed shares or property to charity – and you'll get a double dose of tax relief. If you donate quoted shares, land or buildings, you can reduce your taxable income by the value of the gift and it's exempt from capital gains tax (up to 40 per cent). So if you give shares valued at £20,000, which include a capital gain of £10,000, as a higher rate taxpayer you would save £8,000 on income tax as well as avoid a possible capital gains tax liability of up to £4,000. As a result, the £20,000 gift to charity could effectively cost you just £8,000. That's a pretty generous concession, with the Inland Revenue picking up most of the tab.

Taxpayers can deduct from their income the value of the shares plus any broker's fees and stamp duty incurred in transferring them.

Sharegift is a charity that administers the sale of shares and sends the money raised to any of 300 designated charities. You can give or sell your shares to the Charities Aid Foundation so long as the proceeds less the purchase price paid to the donor exceed £250 and the market value is at least 25 per cent higher than the purchase figure.

Tel: 020 7337 0501
www.sharegift.org.uk

Charities Aid Foundation Charity Account
An easy way to fund a charity habit is to open a Charity Account with the Charities Aid Foundation. You can set up the account by paying in a single amount of £100 or more or by making regular

payments (£10 a month or more) by direct debit. You can also fund your account through Payroll Giving (where you get tax relief at source) or by giving shares. The account acts like a current account for your charitable savings. You get a CharityCard and a 'charity chequebook' that you can use to make donations by post, phone or online whenever you want to a charity of your choice. It's a simple and flexible way of giving.

See **The Charities Aid Foundation** and **The Giving Campaign** above.

Will power

The millions of people who support good causes during their lifetime unfortunately often fail to remember charities in their wills. Although almost 70 per cent of the population donate money during their lifetime, only 4 per cent include a charity in their will. Despite this, however, legacy giving is by far the biggest source of income for charities, with more than £1 billion left to them each year.

Legacies are also the most cost-effective source of income for charities as they can bring in large sums with very little administration involved. Hardly a surprise, then, that virtually all charities promote will-making.

There are tax benefits too. As bequests to charities are exempt from tax, they're not included in the value of your estate and can reduce any inheritance tax bill. Estates valued at more than £263,000 are liable to inheritance tax at 40 per cent. With the rapid rise in property prices over the past few years, many more people are liable to this tax than before. If your estate is worth more than £263,000, a gift to charity in your will could relieve some or all of the tax liability.

So if you don't want to leave your money to the Treasury and prefer to do something more radical or give to causes you are passionate about, make sure you mention this in your will.

The simplest way to donate in your will is to set aside an amount or a particular item for a charity or charities. The only problem with leaving a specific amount is that it will decline in value over the years. What was a generous bequest 20 years ago may not seem like much now. Far better to leave a share or percentage of the residue of your estate, ie what remains of the estate after specific bequests and any debts and administration charges have been paid. That way the charity benefits from any increase in the value of your estate.

Any charity benefiting under your will must be properly named and you must include its registered address. You can't make a general gift to a human-rights charity, for example.

Talk to your solicitor or contact the Remember a Charity campaign, which explains how to help your favourite charity for years to come.

Remember a Charity
Tel: 0808 180 2080
www.rememberacharity.org.uk

You don't have to be rich to leave a donation to charity in your will. As the Remember a Charity campaign says: 'Everyone can leave the world a better place.'

Easy does it

Make sure any donations to charity are made under the Gift Aid scheme

Sign up for monthly Payroll Giving

Leave something to a charity in your will

And painlessly

If you've given till it hurts, or if giving money hurts, there are ways of making donations to charity that are – incredibly – free. To you anyway, as somebody else picks up the tab. So now you've got no excuse.

Plastic fantastic

Did you know that if you changed your credit card, you could help to change the world? And it won't cost you a penny. In fact, your card can actually save lives by helping victims of poverty and repression.

If you spend money using a credit card, a painless way of helping good causes is to swap your card for an 'affinity' credit card. These work in exactly the same way as normal credit cards, except that they make a donation to a named charity when you sign up and every time you spend using the card. There is no annual fee, and the interest rates on the cards are generally competitive.

Charities benefit greatly from the steady stream of income that affinity cards generate. Typically, an affinity card (or rather, the bank issuing it) donates £15 to the charity when you sign up for the card and a further 25p per every £100 you spend. Among the biggest issuers of affinity cards are Bank of Scotland, MBNA and the Co-operative Bank, which has cards for Amnesty International, Oxfam and Greenpeace. Nationwide donates 50p to Comic Relief for every £100 spent on its affinity card.

The Halifax charity card, the biggest in Britain, has raised more than £15 million for charities since its launch in 1988. And there could be a lot more where that came from. According to the Credit Card Research Group, there are just 2.2 million affinity cards in Britain out of a total of 60 million credit cards. Consumer spending on affinity cards was £2.7 billion out of £102 billion spent on credit cards in 2002. A more generous slice of these figures would give a big boost to charity income. So, decide what good cause or causes you want to support and find out if they have an affinity card. Then every time you spend using your card you can bask in a warm glow knowing that you're adding to the millions of pounds raised for charities through this novel method of donation.

The Co-operative Bank
Tel: 0800 591682
www.co-operativebank.co.uk

Nationwide
Tel: 0800 302010
www.nationwide.co.uk

Net benefits

If your heart's in the right place and you have a mouse you can count on, the web has a way to make painless donations to charities. Welcome to 'free cyberphilanthropy'. A number of websites allow you to make a donation that costs you nothing. Organizations fighting hunger, disease and environmental damage are hoping this will prove to be an effective way of raising money and awareness on the internet. You can help to make things better with your mouse by clicking on these sites, where sponsors make a small donation on your behalf for every 'hit', in exchange for advertising. As the United Nations Secretary-General, Kofi Annan, says: 'There are no more excuses... you can now make a difference with the click of a mouse.' So choose a cause you want to support from the list below and get clicking.

Remember that the sponsors make free giving possible and keep these sites in the donation business. So it's a good idea

to visit sponsors' sites once in a while and, who knows, maybe you'll see something you like.

Add these web addresses to your internet 'favourites' and make one of them your homepage, so that it's your first port of click every morning. Besides clicking on these sites every day, you can also help by spreading the word. Let others know that there's an easy way of giving something for nothing.

According to **The Hunger Site**, about a billion people across the world face chronic hunger and 24,000 die every day – of

Did you know...?

Britain currently gives 0.34
per cent of its gross national income
(GNI) in overseas aid.
But this is still less than half
the UN target of 0.70 per cent
to which Britain committed
itself 30 years ago. If all rich countries
met the UN target, it would liberate
$114 billion that could be dedicated
to a serious assault on poverty.
Raising aid to the level of the most
generous country, Denmark, at 1.03
per cent, would release more than
$192 billion.

whom 75 per cent are children. Pretty sobering statistics. Your daily click helps feed the hungry with 1.1 cups of staple food. The site, which is visited by about 220,000 people every day, funded 2,717 tonnes of food in 2002.

www.thehungersite.com

Anti-personnel mines kill or maim more than 26,000 people every year – roughly three people every hour. In about 70 countries, farmland, roads and forests have been made treacherous by anti-personnel landmines. There are estimated to be between 60 million and 100 million landmines laid worldwide, and at the current rate of clearing it will take more than 1,000 years to clear all the mines. Each time you click on the **Clearlandmines** website, donors will give money towards clearing 21 square centimetres of mine-laid terrain.

www.clearlandmines.com

Visitors to **Care2.com** can make free donations to Nature Conservancy, a US-based environmental group, to save/protect the rainforest, oceans and animals. A daily click on the 'Race for the Rainforest', for example, saves 7.6 square metres of forest. The website is visited by a million people every month.

www.care2.com

Listen up

'The trouble with the profit system has always been that it was highly unprofitable to most people'

EB White, US author (1899-1985)

The mother of all click-giving sites allows you to make a 'bulk quick donation' to 10 sites at the same time. It saves a great deal of your click energy as it neatly lines up the sites to which your single click has made a donation. Make sure you wait till all the sites are fully loaded to get the full benefit of your good deed.

www.savingadvice.com/forums/showthread.php?t=109

Phone in

You can also help charities by making the right calls. Sign up with phone companies and internet service providers that make donations at no cost to you. You can even save money while lining charity coffers.

Project Oscar is a phone company that operates in partnership with charities. Individual supporters save money on national and international calls (around 50 per cent compared with BT) while raising funds for good causes. The company donates 15 per cent of the value of your calls to your nominated charity.

Tel: 0800 619 5000
www.projectoscar.org.uk

The Phone Co-op shares its profits with the charities and voluntary organizations that are stakeholders of the co-operative. The co-op is owned by its members. You sign up through a charity, such as the Centre for Alternative Technology, which then receives about six per cent of the cost of your calls.

Tel: 0845 458 9000
www.phonecoop.org.uk

There is no connection or minimum call charge on either of these schemes, and you get to keep your BT line and phone number.

CharityDays is an ISP that makes donations to a charity you nominate (such as Oxfam) when you sign up for one of its internet packages. The amount donated can vary from £1.50 to £10 per month depending on the product you choose, which includes broadband. The prices are competitive, and CharityDays gives 60 per cent of its profits to good causes. Businesses can sign up for the service too.

www.charitydays.net

The **Surefish** ISP and shopping portal is a Christian Aid project. The charity gets money when you surf the net and when you search using the Ask Jeeves search engine.

Tel: 0800 781 7956
www.surefish.co.uk

Post consciousness

A number of charities are happy to receive used stamps, which they can use to raise money. They do this by sorting them (using volunteers, of whom you could be one) and selling in bulk to stamp dealers. They can raise thousands of pounds, and all it takes is a little effort on your part.

So maybe there's a silver lining on that ever-growing cloud of junk mail. While the letters can go straight in the (recycle) bin, the stamps can further a good cause. But don't just stop at your own meagre haul of personal mail. Sign your friends up for stamp collection. At work, stake a claim to the incoming post before envelopes are bin bound. Fan mail is also a big plus in this department, so if you know any famous footballers or rock stars...

Cut the stamps out of the envelopes, making sure you don't damage them. Don't try to peel them off. Then take or send them to the charity you want to support.

If you're a stamp collector, you can donate any duplicates. Or you could donate that entire collection you enthusiastically started as a kid but which has been languishing in the attic for years (or maybe even decades). Your clean-out can help a charity to clean up. Charities can also use postcards, phonecards and foreign banknotes.

Among those that collect stamps are:

Amnesty International
Tel: 020 7814 6200
www.amnesty.org.uk

Oxfam
Tel: 0870 333 2700
www.oxfam.org.uk

Guide Dogs for the Blind
0870 600 2323
www.guidedogs.org.uk

Macmillan Cancer Relief
020 8563 9800
www.macmillan.org.uk

Easy does it

Swap your credit card for
a charity affinity card

Set up a click-giving
website as your home page

Sign up with a phone
company or internet
service provider that
helps charities

Just money

'Money doesn't talk, it swears,' Bob Dylan famously sang. And that's probably because it often finds itself in the unenviable position of supporting a rapacious multinational in its misdeeds or propping up some repressive regime.

Are you appalled by tobacco companies' attempts to boost cigarette sales in the Third World, the role of oil giants in pollution and corruption, and arms sales to repressive governments? You may be surprised to know that your cash could be funding these activities. If you have money in a pension fund, life insurance or an endowment, it's quite likely that some of it has been invested in the tobacco, oil and arms industries. On top of that, your bank may well have lent money to firms whose activities and behaviour you despise.

But you can put a stop to all that by having a say in how your money is spent. And you don't have to be a multi-millionaire to influence your bank, insurance firm or pension fund on their choice of investments.

Give your cash a conscience and then keep it on a tight leash, making sure you know where it is and what it's up to at all times. That's the essence of ethical money. Make your money work for you and, as far as possible, for people in developing countries.

Ethical money looks at companies' social and environmental behaviour – it makes its way towards those that have a positive record and avoids those whose ethics don't stand up to scrutiny. Positive firms are generally those that don't damage the environment, exploit their workforce through low pay and harsh conditions, or make harmful or dangerous products.

Individuals who are voting with their chequebooks already constitute a force to be reckoned with. According to the Co-operative Bank, ethical banking and investment in 2002 added up to more than £7 billion. If your cash isn't part of that figure, now's a good time to do something about it.

Ethical finance encompasses banking, savings, mortgages, insurance and investment. Switching to a bank with ethical credentials is easy; making sure your investments are ethical may take a little more effort.

The Ethical Investment Research Service (Eiris) is a good reference point and a mine of information on ethical finance. It was set up in 1983 by a group of churches and non-governmental organizations (NGOs) that wanted their principles incorporated in their investment strategy.

Ethical Investment Research Service
Tel: 020 7840 5700
www.eiris.org

Banking

Banking on your principles is a good place to start. Eiris has a *Guide to Ethical Banking*, which assesses high-street banks' social and environmental commitments. Check out how (and what) your bank's doing.

The Co-operative Bank is the only overtly ethical institution that offers individuals and companies a full banking service. It takes pride in its squeaky clean image and subjects business customers to a range of ethical tenets. Among other things, it refuses to provide banking services or loans to firms involved in arms or tobacco sales, or to those that damage the environment, have exploitative labour practices or links to repressive governments. The bank turned away about £4 million worth of business in 2002 from companies that failed to meet its ethical criteria. Its stance has boosted profits to record levels, and the bank reckons that a third of its new customers are drawn to it because of its principles.

You can open an account with the Co-op Bank (or its internet alias, Smile) safe in the knowledge that your money won't end up backing dastardly dictators or sweatshop scoundrels. The bank offers current and savings accounts with competitive interest rates. When you switch your account to the Co-op Bank, make sure to tell your previous bankers – in the nicest possible way, of course – that you're leaving them because of their moral turpitude. Here's hoping that one day, in the not-too-distant future, they'll see the light and incorporate some ethics into their money-making.

The Co-operative Bank
Tel: 08457 212212
www.co-operativebank.co.uk

Smile
www.smile.co.uk

Listen up

'It's not people who aren't credit-worthy. It's banks that aren't people-worthy'

Muhammad Yunus, Bangladeshi founder of the Grameen Bank and pioneer of microcredit for the poor

Savings

Ethically minded savers have other options too. Saving with a building society (which has mutual status and is owned by its savers and borrowers) is better than putting your money in a bank. Building societies offer competitive interest rates, are not part of giant multinational conglomerates, and are less likely than banks to loan your hard-earned money to unsavoury businesses.

The Building Societies Association has a list of building societies.

Tel: 020 7437 0655
www.bsa.org.uk

There are some other good homes for your cash. Here, however, your money does good but doesn't attract the best interest rates.

Triodos Bank uses its funds to back businesses that make a difference to society and the environment. It seeks investors who want to put their money to work for positive change. Enterprises it supports include organic farming, renewable energy and fair trade. It offers a full banking service to charities and not-for-profit organizations. Individuals can open savings accounts or tax-efficient mini cash individual savings accounts (ISAs).

For example, it offers a Triodos Amnesty saver account, where it donates a percentage of every pound you deposit to Amnesty. You can also choose to donate all or part of the interest you earn to the human rights organization.

Tel: 0500 008720
www.triodos.co.uk

Charity Bank – a not-for-profit outfit – encourages people to use their savings to provide loans to charities and social enterprises – what it calls 'banking for the common good'. It encourages customers to look to the feelgood factor rather than the financial return. When you deposit money, you're asked to waive all or part of your interest to help boost the bank's lending. Charity Bank makes affordable loans to community and volunteer organizations that find it difficult to borrow from mainstream lenders. According to the bank, as a result of the loans it makes (with your money), these organizations are also able to raise more money elsewhere, leveraging your 'donation' by as much as five times.

Tel: 01732 520029
www.charitybank.org

The Ecology Building Society offers savings accounts and mini cash ISAs. It uses the money deposited with it to help build a more sustainable future by, for example, financing mortgages for energy-efficient housing and rebuilding derelict homes, along with supporting organic farming and eco-businesses. Being a building society, it is owned by its members. It wants its members to share its 'environmental and ecological concerns', and may ask if you are a member of a green organization before it allows you to open an account.

Tel: 0845 674 5566
www.ecology.co.uk

Mortgages

Here, too, the **Co-operative Bank** is an ethical player. And a mortgage from a building society is more ethical than one from a bank.

Look out for the greenhouse effect on ethical mortgages – from the light green of the Co-operative Bank to the dark green of the Ecology Building Soc.

For each new mortgage taken out with the Co-op Bank, it makes an annual donation for the lifetime of the loan to an environmental charity. The bank also gives free advice on making homes more energy efficient.

Norwich & Peterborough Building Society offers a range of green mortgages that includes loans for energy-saving improvements.

Tel: 0845 300 6727
www.npbs.co.uk

The Ecology Building Society's lending policy aims for 'an ecological payback', which means, for example, old properties being renovated, sustainable materials being used and/or energy efficiency being implemented.

www.ecology.co.uk

Insurance

The **Co-operative Insurance Society** (CIS), a sister organization of the Co-op Bank, offers home, motor and travel insurance. It's engaging in a mass consultation with its customers about setting out its ethical policy. In inviting customers to have a say in how their money is used when invested, it wants to know their ethical priorities and views on matters such as global warming, sweatshop labour and animal testing. The results will govern the firm's 'socially responsible' investment policy.

Tel: 08457 464646

www.cis.co.uk

Uniservice is a financial-services company owned by trade unionists for trade unionists. Members of affiliated unions can get home, travel and motor insurance (plus financial and tax advice) through the firm. If you belong to an affiliated union – eg Unifi, Amicus-MSF, NUJ – use the services and help swell its coffers. If not, ask your union to sign up with Uniservice. Any profits will help it to serve members better.

Tel: 01444 419119

www.uniservice.co.uk

Naturesave Policies Ltd provides buildings, contents and travel insurance. Ten per cent of its insurance premiums are deposited in a fund – the Nature Trust – to benefit environmental and conservation projects. The firm also aims to 'encourage

Did you know...?

A tax on cross-border currency transactions (the idea is known as the Tobin Tax) would not only discourage damaging financial speculation but could also transform our world.
If this were set at just 10 cents for every $100 traded, it would raise hundreds of billions of dollars per year which could be channelled by the UN into meeting the basic needs of the world's poor.
www.tobintax.org.uk

the adoption of more environmentally aware trading practices within the business community'. **Naturesave** has commercial policies for businesses, which include a free environmental performance review to help firms become 'greener'. If the recommendations are followed, there is a 10 per cent discount on the premium.

Tel: 01803 864390

www.naturesave.co.uk

The **Environmental Transport Association** campaigns for an environmentally sound and sustainable transport system. It is an environmental alternative to the AA and the RAC, and campaigns against more roads and traffic. The ETA offers car breakdown, motor, home and travel insurance among other benefits for members.

Tel: 0800 212810

www.eta.co.uk

Animal Friends offers pet insurance at competitive rates. It donates all its profits to animal welfare charities such as the RSPCA and Compassion in World Farming.

Tel: 0870 403 0300

www.animalfriends.org.uk

Ethical investment

Can you be a capitalist with a conscience? Some people think ethical investment is an oxymoron. Others that it can be a powerful tool for change.

If you invest in shares, read on about giving them an ethical dimension. If you don't have shares on principle, that's fine. But before you go into denial, consider whether or not you have an endowment, life insurance or a pension. If you are a member

"OF COURSE OUR LENDING CRITERIA ARE SUCH THAT WE WILL HAVE TO ASK YOU A FEW SEARCHING QUESTIONS."

of any of these schemes, I'm afraid you're a shareholder of the companies they choose to invest in. To paraphrase Trotsky very loosely: 'You may not be interested in shares, but shares are interested in you' – particularly in your pension fund.

However, you can use your power as a shareholder – whether direct or indirect – to make companies behave better. Through your investment, you can lean on firms to make sure they don't step out of line.

Investment funds aim to make as much money as possible for their members, and as a result are generally concerned only with a company's financial performance. Ethical funds are also concerned with financial performance, but they look at a company's social and environmental behaviour as well. Studies suggest that you don't have to sacrifice financial performance for your principles – ethical funds often do as well as others. In any case, you can't have a clean conscience with dirty money.

The main tools used by funds engaged in ethical or socially responsible investment are screening and engagement. Negative screening was the initial strategy used, excluding industries such as arms, tobacco, mining or nuclear power. But many people regarded this as too simplistic, and favoured including companies that had positive social and environmental characteristics. Positive screening means companies are chosen because of their good record on, for example, waste management, renewable energy and treatment of workers. The process has evolved further to include a process of engagement – a dialogue with companies. Engagement, or 'responsible shareholding', involves buying shares in a company and steering it towards better social and environmental conduct. This includes raising matters of concern directly with the company's management and/or using voting rights at annual general meetings.

But don't confuse ethical with radical. Among the stalwarts of ethical investments you can find banks, pharmaceutical firms and even oil companies. If you look at the firms listed in some ethical funds, it's sometimes hard not to think the whole thing is a trendy marketing ploy. The word 'ethical' is at times purposely misused by fund managers to attract investors. So although it's hip to have a conscience on investments, watch out for the hype as you put your money where your morals are.

You can, however, choose between 'light green' and 'dark green' investments. Although there are no hard and fast rules as to what is acceptable, the latter is more purist and uses strict negative screening to exclude the corporate bad guys.

As with any funds, there are good, bad and indifferent performers, so you'll have to choose carefully. It's best to go through an independent financial adviser to select an appropriate fund for your money and to find out which firms, in your view, cut the moral mustard.

Eiris (see above) has a list of financial advisers who specialize in ethical investment.

Or try:

Ethical Investors
Tel: 01242 539848
www.ethicalinvestors.co.uk

Ethical Investment Co-operative
Tel: 01748 822402
www.ethicalmoney.org

Pensions

You should know where your investment money is going and what sorts of companies it's supporting. If you're contributing to a pension, it's one of the biggest financial commitments you'll ever make. Pension funds are the largest group of shareholders in the country. This makes them a powerful force in the market, with a great deal of clout over companies. They can have a big say in how these are run, and can set the pace on corporate social responsibility. About 75 per cent of the public say they want their pension companies to take social and environmental concerns into account. However, a number of pension funds and institutional investors – including those of charities, educational and religious institutions, trade unions and local

authorities – continue to hold 'unethical' shares and to take no action to make companies behave more responsibly.

And that's where you come in, beating them about the head (or some more subtle method of persuasion, perhaps) to translate fine principles into practice. Find out about your workplace pension fund's investments, and if you disagree about where the money is going, fight for change. Since July 2000 pension fund trustees have been legally obliged to tell members about their policy on socially responsible investment. They are under no obligation to operate an ethical investment policy, but they must make their position on it clear. As a pension fund member, you can write and ask the trustees what they have done about socially responsible investment.

Also find out about the investment strategy of organizations you have links with – your bank, charities, unions, church groups, etc.

On investment funds and putting pressure on companies to change their behaviour, your voice will be much louder if you link up with others. A number of campaigning groups help shareholders get their claws out for the fat cats.

Eiris has lots of information on its website plus a very good guide: *How Responsible Is Your Pension?*

www.eiris.org

An organization called **Fair Share** helps pension fund members campaign for their funds to be invested ethically. You can register online and support the drive for socially responsible investment.

www.fair-share.org.uk

The **Campaign Against the Arms Trade** names and shames some of the country's biggest investment funds that have money in the arms industry. Its Clean Investment Campaign challenges organizations and lobbies for them to disinvest.

Tel: 020 7281 0297

www.caat.org.uk

Shared benefits

Investors in fair or ethical shares are not just in it for the money. They look more to the social benefits that their cash generates. These investments were once regarded as a charitable donation in all but name. Things have moved on, and some do provide a financial return – but it's certainly not a route to riches. Of course, all the usual health – or wealth – warnings apply, and there are no guarantees about share prices or returns.

However, there appears to be no shortage of people willing to invest their money for the greater good. The country's largest fair trade company, Traidcraft, and the Ethical Property Company were able to raise more than £7 million in 2002 through share issues that were fully subscribed. And investments in renewable energy could enable you to do good and maybe do well at the same time.

Triodos Bank is a good place to start your search for fair shares. It handled the share issues for Cafédirect and the Ethical Property Company. It also runs the Triodos Renewable Energy Fund, which invests in small-scale renewable energy projects. If you want to invest in the fund, Triodos provides a 'matching service' in shares, linking would-be sellers with prospective buyers.

Tel: 0500 008720
www.triodos.co.uk

Thanks to the **Renewable Energy Investment Club**, investing in renewable energy has become a lot easier. Seeking to promote commercial activity in renewable energy, it acts as a broker between investors and projects looking for funds. On joining the club, potential investors are given details of projects in which they may wish to buy shares. The club encourages community-based energy schemes.

Tel: 01654 705000
www.reic.co.uk

Cafédirect raised £5 million through its first share issue in 2004 – the largest ethical public offering (EPO) so far. The company, which put fair trade coffee on the map, has grown rapidly in recent years and now has an annual turnover of £13 million. Share buyers and sellers can register on the matched bargain market run by Triodos.

Tel: 020 7490 9520
www.cafedirect.co.uk

The 19th century French anarchist Pierre-Joseph Proudhon famously said that 'property is theft'. But he never came across the **Ethical Property Company**. It buys and renovates properties, then rents them out at reasonable rates to charities, co-operatives and community organizations. Over the past couple of years the company has paid its shareholders an annual dividend of 3p per share, and there has also been a small increase in the share price. You can register to buy their shares at Triodos's matching service.

Tel: 0845 458 3853
www.ethicalproperty.co.uk

Traidcraft is a limited company that seeks to alleviate poverty in developing countries through trade. It is committed to promoting fair trade, using Christian principles, through concern for people and the environment. Traidcraft sells a large range of fair trade products. The company hasn't paid any dividends to investors so far, but its shares do maintain their value. They can be bought and sold on a matching basis.

Tel: 0191 491 0591

www.traidcraft.co.uk

Shared Interest is a co-operative lending society that provides access to credit – on fair terms – to people in the South who have skills they can use to make a living. Like a building society, it is owned and controlled by its members, who get a vote. Since its launch in 1990 it has funded fair trade projects worth millions of pounds. It pays a small amount of interest, though a number of investors waive their rights to this. You can withdraw your money at any time.

Tel: 0191 233 9100

www.shared-interest.com

Industrial Common Ownership Finance (Icof) has been providing loans to community, co-operative, social and environmental businesses for 30 years. Funds are raised mainly through public share issues. It says shareholders will receive 'dividends where possible, and considerable satisfaction'.

Tel: 020 7251 6181

www.icof.co.uk

Easy does it

**Move your current account to
the Co-operative Bank or Smile**

**Put some of your money into
ethical savings, eg Triodos or
Charity Bank**

**Find out what your pension
fund trustees have done about
socially responsible investment**

Going green

Global warming is here – and now, according to the vast majority of scientists. And ignoring it won't make it go away.

By burning fossil fuels (oil, coal, gas) to produce energy, we release greenhouse gases into the atmosphere, which leads to global warming and climate change. Industrial energy is the biggest culprit, but the energy we use to heat our homes, cook our meals and run our cars pumps out more than 40 per cent of the emissions. Of the gases released, carbon dioxide is the worst offender. It traps the sun's heat in the atmosphere, causing the earth to heat up. The rise in temperature is changing the weather across the world, and is expected to cause more floods and storms as well as drive animals and plants into extinction.

That's the bad news. The good news is that you can do something about it. And without making any great sacrifices.

Overconsumption and waste are contributing to global warming and pollution. So, along with the three 'Rs' you learned at school

– readin' (w)ritin' and (a)rithmetic – there are three more needed for a sustainable planet: reduce (consumption), reuse and recycle. Well, actually, there's a fourth too, which could be a giant leap for humankind: renewable (as in energy).

Although tackling climate change is a battle that must be fought by governments on a global scale, you can play your part. There is great potential to reduce your consumption of fossil fuels, and thus your contribution to global warming. Some of the steps you can take are blindingly obvious and easy, others might need a little more thought and discipline.

The first baby step is to sign up – without further ado – with Friends of the Earth or Greenpeace. These two campaigning organizations are at the forefront of the battle to raise awareness and tackle the planet's environmental problems. Make yourself a part of the search for solutions. They also have a great deal of information on green activities and actions.

Friends of the Earth
Tel: 020 7490 1555
www.foe.co.uk

Greenpeace
Tel: 020 7865 8100
www.greenpeace.org.uk

Saving energy

Britain's energy consumption, in proportion to GDP, is higher than in most European countries. The average household in Britain produces about six tonnes of CO_2 annually from gas and electricity. And running a home generates more CO_2 than running a car.

So don't be energy mad. Save energy, money and the planet at the same time. It's a win-win-win situation.

Start by checking the insulation in your home. If you have cavity walls or lofts that aren't insulated, you could be losing more than 40 per cent of the heat from your home. Also check for draughts from doors and windows. You can seal them using your DIY skills or getting help to put in PVC seals or double glazing. Drawing your curtains at dusk will also help to conserve heat.

Boilers account for about a third of the CO_2 emissions from homes, so make sure that yours is working efficiently. If it's more than 10 years old, it may be time to replace it. An efficient condensing boiler could knock about 40 per cent off your fuel bills. By turning your central heating thermostat down one degree, you could save a further 10 per cent on your gas bill. There's more. Setting the thermostat for your water at 60 degrees centrigrade will provide you with water that's hot, rather than boiling (save that for the kettle) for baths, showers and washing. Putting a jacket on your hot-water tank (and never mind about being fashion conscious) will also help conserve energy. These changes will help to warm your home rather than the planet.

Listen up

'The earth is part of our body, and we never gave up the earth'

Toohoolhoolzote, Native American/Wallowa prophet, 1877.

Buy energy-efficient appliances, which display the 'Energy Efficiency Recommended' logo. This complements the A-G efficiency rating. It's all about making the appliance of science socially responsible. An energy-efficient washing machine uses around half the energy of an inefficient one. And by turning the wash temperature down to 40 degrees rather than 60 degrees you could make big savings. And your clothes will still be clean.

Keep your cool by buying an energy-efficient fridge. Make it even more efficient by not keeping the door open any longer than necessary; defrosting it every couple of months; and waiting till food has cooled before putting it in the fridge.

And while we're in the kitchen: keep the lids on pans when you're cooking (cuts energy use and cooking time), and don't boil more water in the kettle than you are going to use.

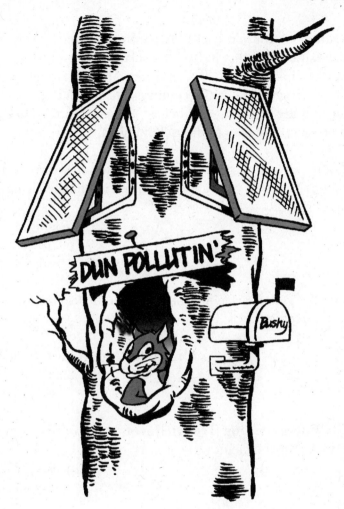

Finally, send out an SOS (Switch Off and Save). Don't leave your TV, stereo, etc on standby – some appliances on standby use up to 70 per cent of the energy they use when switched on. Unplug mobile phone chargers when you've recharged your phone. And when you leave a room, switch the lights off.

Meanwhile, switch on to energy-saving light bulbs. They cost more than ordinary bulbs but last a lot longer and use a fraction of the electricity. According to the Energy Saving Trust, if every home in Britain replaced three of its bulbs with energy-efficient ones, it would save enough energy to power all the streetlights in the country. That would save tonnes of harmful greenhouse gases being released into the atmosphere (and loads of money off household bills).

If, after all of the above, you want to go a step further to clear your conscience, you can get involved in climate change campaigning.

Rising Tide UK
Tel: 01865 241097
www.risingtide.org.uk

Or see if your household can rise up to the Centre for Alternative Technology's 'Carbon Challenge'

Centre for Alternative Technology
Tel: 01654 705950
www.cat.org.uk

The **Energy Saving Trust** tells you how to make your home more energy efficient.

Tel: 020 7222 0101
www.est.co.uk

Alternatively, contact your local **Energy Efficiency Advice Centre**.

Tel: 0800 512012

Action Energy helps businesses to cut energy costs. It gives free advice and practical help (such as interest-free loans).

Tel: 0800 585794
www.actionenergy.org.uk

Did you know...?

The recommended basic
water requirement per person
per day is 50 litres – though people
can get by with 5 litres
for drinking and cooking and
25 for washing.
The average British citizen uses
200 litres a day, the
average American 500 litres.
The average Malian, meanwhile,
has to get by with just 8 litres
a day and the average Gambian
with just 4.5 litres.

Renewable energy

Renewable energy – clean, green power – could provide a long-term solution to global warming. For example, Britain has the richest wind-energy resource in Europe, which could generate almost three times the current demand for electricity. The 'fuel' for wind power is free, the supply is unlimited, and no nasty gases are released when the energy is generated. Yet less than four per cent of the country's electricity supply relies on renewable energy.

Energy from the sun is also clean and free, and can be harnessed to generate electricity and heat water in your home.

Power companies are – slowly – starting to come on board about green energy. Since April 2002 all electricity suppliers have had to buy or generate at least three per cent of their power from green sources. Some suppliers go well beyond the minimum, and there are 100 per cent good guys.

By switching to green energy you're helping to fight global warming and taking a step towards future sustainability. And the more demand there is, the more supply will be created, having a positive impact on prices. Friends of the Earth has a list of recommended green suppliers. One of their top choices is **Good Energy** (formerly Unit[e]).

Tel: 0845 456 1640
www.good-energy.co.uk

Greenpeace has teamed up with the energy supplier npower to develop **Juice**.

Tel: 0845 120 2755
www.npower.com/juice

Both Good Energy and Juice supply 100 per cent green power. Switching from your existing supplier should be easy, and you'll continue to receive your electricity through the existing network. Good Energy costs a little more (£2-£3 a month above your current tariff) because it doesn't have the economies of scale of the giant npower (the country's biggest electricity supplier), which also produces energy from fossil fuels. Juice will cost you no more (and maybe less) than you're currently paying for electricity. Renewable energy can be used for businesses as well. Switch to green energy at work and play, and it's guaranteed to double your moral satisfaction. Good Energy supplies businesses with green power, but npower reverts to fossil fuels for its business customers.

You can also go power mad and generate your own energy. Although Britain's weather falls far short of the dreams of sun worshippers, it's good enough to generate solar power – which doesn't need sunshine, just daylight. Solar-powered garden lighting is available and easy to use. The cost of installing solar panels to generate energy for your home is still quite high, but grants are available for up to 50 per cent of the cost. For details:

Energy Saving Trust
Tel: 020 7222 0101
www.est.org.uk

Solar Century
Tel: 020 7803 0100
www.solarcentury.co.uk

To ensure that clean energy comes into its own, you can lobby your MP and local council leaders about reducing greenhouse gas emissions. And add your voice to campaigns by Friends of the Earth and Greenpeace. On top of that, you can invest in renewables (see the *Just money* chapter on ethical investment).

Cars

Poll after poll shows car owners think that reducing car use is a great idea – for other car owners.

If you're a car user, try cutting down on short journeys. Walking will save on emissions and get you healthier in the bargain.

Use public transport when you can. You'll probably get to

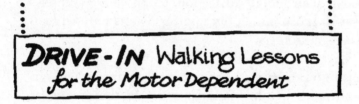

where you want to go faster, and so will everybody else if there are fewer cars on the roads.

If you're doing school runs by car, try and avoid the massive amounts of petrol used and pollution caused, not to mention the horrendous traffic jams, by instituting supervised, collective walking or use of public transport to school.

Car sharing is another step forward. For commuters, it'll reduce car costs, save wear and tear on your car, and cut driving stress levels during the week.

Liftshare is a widely used website that helps people find drivers and passengers online. It also has a site (school-run. org) to enable parents to share the school run.

Tel: 08700 111199
www.liftshare.com

Share a Journey organizes corporate membership to promote car sharing. It also aims to help with the school run.

www.shareajourney.com

Joining a car club is another way of making car ownership cheaper and helping to cut down on greenhouse gas emissions.

Tel: 0113 234 9299
www.carclubs.org.uk

The **Environmental Transport Agency** promotes sensible and responsible motoring, and is a green alternative to other motoring organizations. Sign up for its motor and breakdown insurance, and you'll be contributing to the campaign for a sustainable transport system. The ETA also gives advice on fuel-efficient cars and publishes a guide.

Tel: 0800 212810
www.eta.co.uk

If all those who drive to work used alternative transport just once a week, it would cut road traffic by a fifth, and CO_2 emissions from traffic by more than 10 per cent. Surely that can't be so hard to do.

Sustrans is a sustainable transport charity that works on practical projects to encourage people to walk, cycle and use public transport in order to reduce motor traffic and its adverse effects.

Tel: 0845 113 0065

www.sustrans.org.uk

Sustrans also runs a **Safe Routes to Schools** campaign, which you can reach at:

www.saferoutestoschools.org.uk

Bicycles

Pedal power is green, healthy and saves you money – on fares and on the gym membership you'll no longer need. If you cycle to work, you're getting good, outdoor exercise on the way there (and back) and will eventually recoup the cost of your bike through saved fares. If you're new to regular cycling, start off by buying a bike at the lower end of the scale. Once you've decided that you definitely want to belong to the bike community, you can move up to a more sophisticated model. At that stage you'll really appreciate the upgrade as you speed through the urban jungle leaving cars in your wake – screaming something like 'So long suckers!' And you can donate your old bike to Re-Cycle.

Re-Cycle

Tel: 0845 458 0854

www.re-cycle.org

It's well worth joining the **Cyclists' Touring Club**, the national cyclists' organization. It's a one-stop shop for everything to do with cycling: advice, information, insurance, a magazine, tours, events, etc. On top of that it has a shop for bikes and accessories (including clothing). As a member you're automatically insured against claims for injury or damage (in case of an accident).

Tel: 0870 873 0060
www.ctc.org.uk

Bicycle User Groups (handily known as BUGs) are proliferating all across Britain; so too are Cycle Campaign Groups. Some have successfully campaigned to have employers install showers to encourage cycle-commuting. There is a list of British BUGs and campaign groups at the **Cycle Campaign Network**.

www.cyclenetwork.org.uk

Water

Water is a precious commodity, as only one per cent of the world's water is available for use. Yet we waste huge amounts every day through leakage, evaporation and contamination. It's even been predicted that future wars will be fought over water rather than oil.

At home, make sure every drop counts. To save water, you don't have to shower with a friend – though that can be fun sometimes. Taking a shower instead of a bath is already a step in the right direction. A shower uses just 40 per cent of the hot water needed for a bath, and you save on energy too.

And though it may not be as sexy as putting a tiger in your tank, putting a Hippo in your cistern does a lot more good. Most toilets don't need a full cistern to flush effectively, and a Hippo

can save up to three litres of water per flush. If a Hippo is too big for your cistern, try a Save-a-flush, which saves about a litre per flush. They're both usually available from your local water supplier.

Since a toilet is flushed about five times a day, a Hippo could save you a staggering 5,500 litres annually. However, if you already have a clever dual-flush toilet, you're ahead of the game and don't need to introduce any foreign bodies into your cistern.

Don't leave the water running when you brush your teeth or shave – even if it means changing the bad habits of a lifetime. And get leaking taps fixed as soon as possible – you can waste up to 90 litres a week.

If you've got the space, a water butt in your garden or patio can be used to collect rainwater, which you can use on your plants and lawn. A 220-litre butt costs about £35.

Check out the Thames Water website for water saving ideas and water butts.

www.thameswateruk.co.uk

You can also contribute to helping others sort out their water problems. More than one billion people worldwide live without clean water, and more than two billion have no proper sanitation. **Water Aid** works to get water, sanitation and hygiene education to some of the poorest people in the world. Think of the money you've saved by tightening up on you energy and water use, and recycle some of it into a (tax-efficient) donation.

Tel: 020 7793 4500

www.wateraid.org

Easy does it

**Switch off the standby on
your TV and stereo overnight**

**Have at least one car-free day
a week — use public transport,
cycle or walk instead**

**Take a shower rather than a bath
and put a Hippo in your cistern**

Talkin' trash

Every household in Britain produces more than a tonne of waste annually. That's a waste mountain of about 28 million tonnes altogether. Almost 80 per cent of this is buried in landfill sites, which pollutes ground water and produces gases that contribute to global warming. Although up to 80 per cent of that waste can be recycled or composted, we are slackers compared with our European neighbours. Britain recycles about 12 per cent, while Austria reaches a giddy high of more than 60 per cent.

It's time to clean up our act. Each of us (yes, that means you) needs to do something about the amount of waste we generate. This is where the aforementioned three Rs come into their own. Only by seriously reducing, reusing and recycling will we be able to make a dent in that ever-growing waste mountain.

Reducing consumption and thus throwing away less is the best solution to the problem. Not making waste is the most environmentally friendly way to deal with it. So think about what you're buying and aim for minimal packaging (and let manufacturers know when they're overdoing it). It also means doing little things like using a mug for drinks at work rather than a styrofoam cup.

Reuse items as far as possible. If something's broken and can be fixed, get it fixed rather than replacing it. If you're replacing computers, stereos or washing machines that still work, donate them to a project that refurbishes and recycles them. Don't just chuck out old clothes and toys, give them to a charity. Re-

ON A CLEAR DAY YOU CAN SEE WASTE MOUNTAINS IN THE U.K.

using is better than recycling because items don't need to be reprocessed (which uses up energy and materials).

Recycling and composting will help keep your waste to a minimum. Some items (like bottles and paper) can be easily recycled, and many councils now pick them up from your doorstep. Others, such as cardboard and plastic bottles, need to be taken to your nearest recycling plant. If your council only provides minimal recycling facilities, make a fuss for it to provide more.

And buy recycled products where possible, to loop the loop and make the whole recycling process a success. As demand for recycled products increases, more will be produced, which means more waste can be recycled.

Waste Watch promotes and encourages action on the three Rs. And its Business Network helps businesses to cut waste, saving money and the environment. It also has information on products made from recycled materials.

Tel: 020 7089 2100
www.wastewatch.org.uk

Recycled Products provides a guide to products that contain recycled materials.

www.recycledproducts.org.uk

Compost

Composting will help to reduce your waste line more than any other method of recycling – up to 60 per cent of what's in your bin can be recycled naturally. Kitchen and garden waste (fruit and vegetable waste, grass, leaves, etc) can do the business in a compost bin along with paper and cardboard such as envelopes, tissues, kitchen- and toilet-roll centres, and egg boxes. Subsidized compost bins are often available through local councils, or you can buy them at garden centres.

Composting is an all-round winner: it saves on waste disposal costs; gives you a free supply of compost for your plants and garden; and saves peat bogs, which are habitats for wildlife.

Two good websites tell you pretty much everything you wanted to know about home composting but were afraid to ask.

North Derbyshire Home Composting Project
www.compost-it.org.uk

California's **Alameda County Waste Management Authority** points out how to 'do the rot thing'.

www.stopwaste.org

Paper

Each person in the country uses about six trees' worth of paper a year, putting pressure on forests across the world. Making paper also uses lots of energy, water and chemicals. And we're not good about recycling. Paper makes up about a quarter of household rubbish, but less than half of it is recycled.

Try and use less 'virgin' paper (that's the gleaming white stuff). Set high standards by sending email greetings cards, or (charity) cards printed on recycled paper. With millions of Christmas cards being sent every year, using ones printed on non-recycled paper should be regarded as eco-vandalism.

Unfortunately, the much-talked-about paperless office is still only a virtual reality. Help it to come about by not printing documents unless you have to. Printing emails, for example, is

a definite no-no. When photocopying and printing, try to use both sides of the paper.

Curb the rampant flow of junk mail. Britons receive more than four billion pieces of direct mail every year, as a result of which almost 80,000 tonnes of paper ends up in landfill. Make sure you recycle your unwanted mail, but better than that, register free of charge with the **Mailing Preference Service**. It'll get your name taken off 95 per cent of mailing lists.

Tel: 020 7291 3310

www.mpsonline.org.uk

Did you know...?

If everyone in the world was as wasteful as we are in Britain, we would need eight worlds just to keep going.

Reuse paper as far as possible – as rough paper, doodle-pads, phone-message notepaper and so on.

Then recycle: for every tonne of paper recycled, you'll save 17 trees, 3.33kh/hours of energy and five cubic metres of landfill space.

Buy recycled paper. It uses only about half the energy needed to make virgin paper and a lot less water and chemicals. And don't forget recycled toilet paper. There's no good argument for not using it.

Recycled paper products are now available in most supermarkets and high street shops. If you have trouble finding them, make sure you ask at shops to encourage them to stock up.

Don't stop there. Push the publications you read towards using environmentally friendly paper – either recycled or certified by the Forest Stewardship Council. Let them know that you're a regular reader who's concerned about the environmental impact of not using sustainable sources.

Remarkable produces a truly remarkable range of environmentally friendly stationery. Check out its award-winning pencil made from a recycled plastic vending cup (how cool is that). Its website lists shops that sell its products.

www.remarkable.co.uk

Recycled paper can be had from:

Paperback
Tel: 020 8980 5580
www.paperback.coop

Recycled Paper Supplies
Tel: 01676 533832
www.recycled-paper.co.uk

You can also reuse envelopes. Spread the word about Amnesty International or Friends of the Earth and save trees at the same time by using their address labels to stick on the envelopes you reuse.

Amnesty International
(£2 for 50 labels)
Tel: 01285 750466

Friends of the Earth
(£2.50 for 100)
Tel: 020 7490 1555

Nappies

About three billion (yes, that's billion) disposable nappies make their way into landfill sites every year. They cost huge amounts of money to dispose of, occupy vast acres of land, and can take up to 500 years to decompose (while emitting noxious gases). Not a pretty picture.

Reusable nappies don't cost the earth (in more ways than one), are just as easy to use as disposables, and will halve your rubbish instantly. And you don't have to wash them yourself, as nappy laundry services are now available in most areas. For more information on the real things, see below and/or ask your local council.

The **Real Nappy Association** has a list of retailers, laundries, etc across the country.

Tel: 020 7481 9004
www.realnappy.com

For a list of nappy washers in your area, contact the **National Association of Nappy Services**.

Tel: 0121 6934949
www.changeanappy.co.uk

Plastic

Plastic packaging, bottles and bags are a scourge of our all-consuming times. Households generate about a million tonnes of packaging waste annually. Avoid it when you can. Write to firms that are over-packaging their products and let them know you're unhappy with their cavalier treatment of the environment.

We use 15 million plastic bottles every day, and – despite the fact that they take hundreds of years to biodegrade – we only recycle about four per cent. Make yourself part of the effort to boost that recycling figure. If your council doesn't recycle plastic bottles, put pressure on them to provide facilities.

The billions of plastic bags we use are choking the planet. Some countries have banned them, while others have imposed a tax. Ireland has introduced a 15 cent tax per bag, which has drastically curbed their use (by more than 90 per cent). Always take bags with you when you go shopping so that you can use them again and again. When they can no longer be used, recycle

them. Better still, use mesh and string bags, or sturdy hemp and (organic) cotton ones.

However, biodegradable bags are on the way. They decompose when exposed to air and can be composted (if that really works, this paragraph will self-destruct).

Beyond the basics

OK, so you've recycled every newspaper, baked-bean can and wine bottle that you brought home. And you've trudged to your local recycling plant with your cardboard and plastic bottles (of course, after reusing some of them first). Maybe you're composting, too, and disposable nappies no long-er (dis)grace your baby's bottom. Well done. Take a bow. Environmental angel status beckons.

If you're able and willing, take it further. Ask at your work canteen and at your favourite pubs and restaurants if they re-cycle (glass, at least). And then go beyond recycling just the usual suspects. Here's a far from exhaustive list of some of the things that can be guided towards recycle heaven. Many can also be recycled at your local council recycling plant (if it's a forward-thinking council, that is).

Batteries

About 25,000 tonnes of household batteries are bought in Britain every year, of which less than 1,000 tonnes are recycled. Some of the toxic materials have now been removed from batteries, but the heavy metals they contain can still cause pollution problems when they're dumped in landfill sites. Unfortunately, very few councils offer collection and/or recy-cling facilities for household batteries – but check with yours in case it's one of the pioneers. Use rechargeable nickel cadmium batteries as far as possible, although these do contain cadmium, which is highly toxic. However, a number of manufacturers of rechargeables (Eveready among them) accept the return of their batteries, which they send for recycling. You can also buy wind-up radios and torches, and solar-powered lights. A number of councils accept car batteries for recycling, as do some local garages.

Bicycles

Re-Cycle is an award-winning charity that renovates unwanted cycles and ships them abroad. Instead of letting your old two-wheel wonder rust away, help it find a good home elsewhere. Re-Cycle also seeks donations to help with its work.

Tel: 0845 458 0854

www.re-cycle.org

Books

Almost all charities accept books. **Amnesty** runs a string of second-hand bookshops, where you can donate your old books and buy someone else's.

Tel: 020 7814 6292

Clothes/textiles

Every year Britons add about a million tonnes of old clothes to their rubbish pile. Practically all of that could be recycled and given a new lease of life. Happily, a further 200,000 tonnes are recycled – either to be worn again or used in industry.

Have a look through your wardrobe and if there're any clothes you haven't worn for a year, think about giving them to charity. As Marx said, 'The more you have, the less you are.' Or was it the other way round?

Oxfam is one of many charities that's big on reselling clothes. You can deliver to local branches or put in clothes banks. Old clothes and other textiles can also be recycled (rather than re-used) – check at your local recycling plant or try **Traid** (Textile Recycling for Aid and International Development).

Tel: 020 8733 2580
www.traid.org.uk

Computers

The voracious appetite for buying new computers is bad news for the environment. A Japanese study says that every new computer uses about 240kg of fossil fuels, 22kg of chemicals and 1,500kg of water. Then, at the end of their short lives, about 90 per cent of old computer equipment – much of it still in working order – is dumped in landfill sites. But you can help to bring down the high price paid for this planned obsolescence.

Don't be in such a hurry to upgrade, give your old computer to someone who can use it – in Britain or in the South – and buy a refurbished rather than a brand new machine.

Computer Aid International helps to bridge the global digital divide by recycling donated computers for use in schools and community organizations in the developing world. You can also sponsor its work.

Tel: 020 7281 0091
www.computer-aid.org

Computers for Charity aims to promote IT use by community groups here and abroad.

Tel: 01288 361199
www.computersforcharity.org.uk

Refurbished computers can be had from:

Natural Collection
Tel: 0870 331 3333
www.naturalcollection.com

Uniservice (for union members)
Tel: 01444 419713

Listen up

'Human society sustains itself by transforming nature into garbage'

Mason Cooley, contemporary US aphorist

Furniture

Reusing furniture and domestic appliances diverts vast quantities of waste from landfill sites.

The **Furniture Reuse Network** is an umbrella organization for furniture recycling projects across the country. It provides low-income families with second-hand furniture and appliances.

Tel: 01924 375252
www.frn.org.uk

Green-works is a not-for-profit organization that gives businesses an environmentally friendly way of disposing of their office furniture (and makes a profit in the bargain). Old furniture can be donated to the firm, which then sells it on cheaply to charities, schools and community groups.

Tel: 020 7401 5409
www.green-works.co.uk

Ink cartridges

About 40 million ink cartridges from printers, faxes and photocopiers are thrown away every year. You can reduce the waste caused by their production and disposal and, at the same time, raise money for good causes. Donate used cartridges to Oxfam or ActionAid, which are in partnership with firms that refurbish and sell them. The charities can make between £1.50 and £10 per cartridge. Make sure you buy recycled cartridges to keep the process moving along nicely.

Oxfam
Tel: 01873 859901
www.oxfam.org.uk

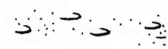

ActionAid
Tel: 0845 3100200
www.actionaid.org.uk

Cartridges for Charity
Tel: 0845 121 0674
www.cartridges4charity.co.uk

Mobile phones

There are millions of unloved mobile phones lying around
in homes and offices waiting for someone to call. If they're
dumped in landfill sites, they leak chemicals and pollute the
soil. They can, instead, be reused in eastern Europe and the
developing world. And they can help make money for a charity
on their way there. So make sure you hand over your handset
to the right people. You could also organize a collection among
friends and at work to give the phones a new lease of life.

A number of charities collect phones for reuse and recycling. They can be dropped off (at Oxfam shops, for example), you can mail them in free or, if you have lots, have them picked up. The charity gets, on average, about £5 for each phone, but can get quite a lot more depending on condition and model.

Oxfam
Tel: 0870 752 0999
www.oxfam.org.uk/mobile

ActionAid
Tel: 0845 310 0200
www.actionaid.org.uk

Childline
Tel: 020 7650 3200
www.childline.org.uk

Tools

Put your old tools to good use in Africa. **Tools for Self Reliance** provides refurbished tools and skills training to local organizations in African countries. Check its website to see what tools it needs. It also accepts donations to help with its work.

Tel: 023 8086 9697
www.tfsr.org

And finally, a couple of good reference sources for would-be eco warriors.

Green Guide is a comprehensive directory for organic living, teeming with useful information. It produces regional editions.

Tel: 01970 613000
www.greenguideonline.com

Green Choices is a user-friendly website that tells you all about things green.

www.greenchoices.org

Easy does it

Switch at least three bulbs at home to energy-efficient ones

Buy Christmas cards made with recycled paper (or email greetings)

Make sure your old mobile phone gets recycled via a charity

Reading for the part

'To know and not to act is not really to know,' according to the Chinese philosopher Wang Yang-ming (1472-1529). By reading some of the publications and visiting some of the websites listed here, you can make sure you know – so that you can act.

To boost the coffers of progressive publications, subscribe rather than buy off the shelf. This will help to ensure that they have money in hand to plan ahead, advertise to boost circulation, and continue to give you more of whatever it is you like about them in the first place. As the US-based *The Nation* magazine says: 'You need to subscribe to more than our principles.'

Also make sure the rest of the world (well, your friends at least) is on message by spreading the word about these magazines. And ask for them at your local library – if they aren't available, see if they can take out a subscription.

Magazines

Corporate Watch
Keeps tabs on and supports activism against large corporations. 'The earth is not dying, it is being killed, and those who are killing it have names and addresses.'
Bimonthly, £8
16b Cherwell Street
Oxford OX4 IBG
Tel: 01865 791391
www.corporatewatch.org.uk

Direct Action
Radical ideas and action.
Quarterly, £5
PO Box 29, South West PDO
Manchester M15 5HW
Tel: 07984 675281
www.direct-action.org.uk

The Ecologist
'The world's most widely read environmental magazine.'
10 issues, £28
Ecosystems Limited
Unit 18, Chelsea Wharf
15 Lots Road
London SW10 0QJ
Tel: 01795 414963
www.theecologist.org

Ergo
Published by Global Action Plan, which is committed to finding practical solutions to environmental and social problems.
Quarterly, £14
Global Action Plan
8 Fulwood Place
London WC1V 6HG
Tel: 020 7405 5633
www.ergo-living.com

Ethical Consumer
Guide to shopping with a conscience, published by the Ethical Consumer Research Association.
Bimonthly, £19
Unit 21
41 Old Birley Street
Manchester M15 5RF
Tel: 0161 226 2929
www.ethicalconsumer.org

Focus on Africa
Magazine of the BBC African Service, covers politics, business and culture.
Quarterly, £14
Bush House
PO Box 76
London WC2 4PH
Tel: 01442 879097
www.bbcworldservice.com/focus

The Guardian Weekly
International edition of the daily *Guardian* with articles from the *Observer* and pages from the *Washington Post* and *Le Monde*.
Weekly, £64
75 Farringdon Road
London EC2N 3HQ
Tel: 0870 066 0510
www.guardianweekly.co.uk

Index on Censorship
'For free expression.'
Quarterly, £32 (224pp)
33 Islington High Street
London N1 9LH.
Tel: 020 7278 2313
www.indexonline.org

Le Monde Diplomatique
Edited English translation of high-brow, progressive French paper.
Monthly, £36
Tel: 020 7288 2222
www.mondediplo.com

London Review of Books
Lively, radical, literary magazine.
Fortnightly, £34 (special offers available)
28 Little Russell Street
London WC1A 2HN
Tel: 020 7209 1101
www.lrb.co.uk

Middle East International
Intelligent, authoritative and
independent.
Fortnightly, £85
1 Gough Square
London EC4A 3DE
Tel: 020 7832 1333
http://meionline.com

**Nacla: Report on the
Americas**
'The most widely read
English language publication
on Latin America.' Published
by the North American
Congress on Latin America
Bi-monthly, £25
Order from:
Latin America Bureau
1 Amwell Street
London EC1R 1UL
Tel: 020 7278 2829
www.lab.org.uk
www.nacla.org

The Nation
Good, progressive writing on
US and international issues.
Weekly, $95 (airmail)
33 Irving Place
New York, NY 10003,
US
Tel: 001 212 209 5400
www.thenation.com

New Consumer
'Fair trade magazine: making
shopping matter.'
Bimonthly, £10
14 Albany Street
Edinburgh EH1 3QB
Tel: 0131 561 1780
www.newconsumer.org

New Internationalist
'The people, the ideas, the
action in the fight for global
justice.'
Monthly, £28.85
55 Rectory Road
Oxford OX4 1BW
Tel: 01858 438896
www.newint.org

New Statesman
Leftwing political and
cultural magazine.
Weekly, £70 (special offers
available)
52 Grosvenor Gardens
London SW1W 0AU
Tel: 020 7730 3444
www.newstatesman.com

Did you know...?

Around 30,000 children die each day from easily preventable illnesses. The number of children killed by diarrhoea in the 1990s is greater than the total number of people who have died in armed conflict since World War Two.

New Left Review
Heavyweight journal of the
international left.
Bimonthly, £32 (160pp)
6 Meard Street
London W1F 0EG
Tel: 020 7434 1210
www.newleftreview.net

Orbit
'Global development issues
through the eyes of the
people who've experienced
them.' Published by
Voluntary Service Overseas.
3 times a year, £15
317 Putney Bridge Road
London SW15 2PN
Tel: 020 7780 7200
www.vso.org.uk/orbit

Red Pepper
'Independent magazine of the
green and radical left.'
Monthly, £22
1b Waterlow Road
London N19 5NJ
Tel: 020 7281 7024
www.redpepper.org.uk

Race & Class
'A journal on racism, empire
and globalization.' Published by
the Institute of Race Relations.
Quarterly, £24
Institute of Race Relations
2-6 Leeke Street
London WC1X 9HS
Tel: 020 7837 0041
www.irr.org.uk/publication/
raceandclass/

Resurgence
'An international forum
for ecological and spiritual
thinking.'
Bimonthly, £21
Ford House, Hartland,
Bideford, Devon EX39 6EE
Tel: 01237 441293
www.resurgence.org

Searchlight
Anti-fascist magazine that
shines a light on the far right.
Monthly, £24
PO Box 1576
Ilford IG5 0NG
Tel: 020 7681 8660
www.searchlightmagazine.com

Most of these magazines can be ordered at reduced rates online through the **Independent News Collective**, a trade association of the radical and alternative press in the UK. It has more than 70 member publications.

www.ink.uk.com

Listen up

'Humans cannot live on earth unless they have a little bit of heaven in mind or heart'

Phil Bosmans, contemporary Belgian priest

Books

The **Wellred** website provides 'good reading for radicals'. It recommends progressive books, which are listed according to geographic areas and countries. Includes fiction and non-fiction. A good place to start if you're interested in or are visiting a country and want to read up about it. You can buy books through the site, and can recommend books that you think ought to be listed.

www.wellred.co.uk

Buy your books in independent bookshops, as far as possible, to ensure that alternatives remain to the ever-encroaching chains. And if they're progressive bookshops, so much the better. If they don't have the books you want in stock, they can almost always order them – at no extra cost to you.

Here are a few recommended bookshops:

Bookmarks
1 Bloomsbury Street
London WC1
Tel: 020 7637 1848
www.bookmarks.uk.com

Housman's
5 Caledonian Road
London N1
Tel: 020 7837 4473

London Review Bookshop
14 Bury Place
London WC1
Tel: 020 7269 9030
www.lrb.co.uk/lrbshop

Greenleaf Bookshop
82 Colston Street
Bristol BS1 5BB
Tel: 0117 9211369
www.greenleafbookshop.co.uk

News From Nowhere
96 Bold Street
Liverpool L1 4HY
Tel: 0151 7087270
www.newsfromnowhere.org.uk

Word Power Bookshop
43 West Nicholson Street
Edinburgh EH8 9DB
Tel: 0131 6629112
www.word-power.co.uk

For a list of other progressive bookshops, see:
www.schnews.org.uk/pap/bookshops.htm

Web wisdom

BBC News is one of the best sites for up-to-date news and features from around the world. You can also catch up with radio programmes that you've missed.

www.bbcnews.com

The Institute for Global Communications This grandly titled organization seeks to further the work of progressive groups and individuals for social justice and sustainability through the internet. It has anti-racism, eco, women's and peace sections.

www.igc.org

Inter Press Service has information on global issues provided by a network of journalists in more than 100 countries. Daily news and features on politics, development, environment, human rights, etc.

www.ips.org

OneWorld has a vast amount of information, which includes news and reports on Third World and development issues, plus links to NGOs, jobs and more.

www.oneworld.net

Panos works with journalists from the South to produce news, features and analysis of global issues.

www.panos.org.uk

Z Magazine Online – Znet consists of a community of people committed to social change, where 'the spirit of resistance lives'. It's an enormous site brimming with interesting information.

www.zmag.org

Other voices

The **Africa Centre** promotes awareness about Africa. It organizes talks, conferences, workshops and cultural events, and has a library and a bookshop. Membership costs £20 annually.

> 38 King Street
> London WC2
> Tel: 020 7836 1973
> www.africacentre.org.uk

In 2003, the **Development Studies Association** launched an online guide to development studies courses at universities. The guide features about 40 centres that offer undergraduate, postgraduate and short courses. As well as information on the courses, the site has links to the institutions listed.

> www.devstud.org.uk/courseguide

Latin America Bureau is a research and publishing organization that seeks to raise awareness and promote understanding of Latin American issues. It has produced a number of books on the region; its website provides links to a wealth of information; and it runs courses in London. You can join as a supporter for £20, which entitles you to a free country guide book, a 25 per cent discount on LAB books, and mailings about books and events.

> Tel: 020 7278 2829
> www.lab.org.uk

The **Minority Rights Group** works to protect the rights of minorities and indigenous people worldwide. It has published a number of well-researched reports. As a subscriber (£40), you'll get six reports and profiles, a regular e-bulletin and an annual report.

> Tel: 020 7422 4200
> www.minorityrights.org

The **New Economics Foundation** is an independent think-and do-tank that looks for radical solutions to the planet's problems. It puts people and the planet first. Its website has information and news, and tells you how you can get involved in bringing about change.

Tel: 020 7820 6300
www.neweconomics.org

Easy does it

Take out a subscription to a progressive magazine

Support your local independent bookshop

Check out some of the alternative information sources available on the web

Seeing red

So you've done good – from ethical consumption to going green – and feel good about it. But now the blood is pumping, you're seeing red, and you're all fired up to do more. Well, read on, there's a lot more that you can do.

Parliamentary procedures

Voting in elections should definitely figure on your 'to-do' list. If you want to show you're unhappy or that no party represents you, by all means spoil your ballot paper. If you don't vote, the powers that be will never know how you feel – and every party will find an answer for your non-participation that suits them.

Whether you voted for your local MP or not, he or she still represents you. You can write to or lobby them about unfair international trading rules, protecting the environment, wind energy, weapons of mass destruction you may have found or any other bee you might have in your bonnet (but make sure it's important). The websites below have useful information on when your MP can help you, how to submit a petition and how to get his or her attention.

You can get your MP's name and fax number from the House of Commons Information Unit.

Tel: 020 72194272

Or by visiting:

www.locata.co.uk/commons

You can email your MP from the site.

FaxYourMP.com does a lot of the legwork for you. You enter your postcode and up comes information about your MP along with a fax form. You type in your message, your name and address, and your email address. It emails you to check that you

want to send a fax to your MP, and when you confirm this it sends the fax. You may think it a bit naff sending a fax in this day and age, but the truth is that many MPs are on the wrong side of the digital divide and computers are alien to them (well, almost). Faxes are also harder to ignore, compared with an email lying unnoticed in your inbox.

You can, of course, also write to your MP at:

> House of Commons
> London SW1A 0AA

The Guardian website has information about your MP's surgery and voting record: Ask Aristotle is a political database packed with information.

> www.politics.guardian.co.uk

To find out about your MEP:

> Tel: 020 7227 4300
> www.europarl.org.uk

Campaign strategy

Join organizations that are campaigning to make the world a better place. Your time, money and effort will make a difference.

Amnesty International
Amnesty works to defend human rights worldwide. As a member, you can write letters on behalf of political prisoners, campaign, raise money (plus take out an Amnesty Visa card) and lobby your MP.

> Tel: 020 7814 6200
> www.amnesty.org.uk

If you're too busy to write or have letter-writers' block, fear not, help is at hand. Amnesty appeal letters can be downloaded from the internet or ordered by post.

Appeals Worldwide
51 Fore Street, Totnes TQ9 5NJ
www.appealsww.com

Refugee Action helps refugees and asylum seekers to build new lives in Britain. It aims to build 'a society in which refugees are welcome, respected and safe'. You can help with donations, fundraising and corporate support, and by volunteering. You may also find that your town has an organization that works with refugees.

Tel: 020 7654 7700
www.refugee-action.org

World Development Movement
WDM seeks justice for the world's poor and campaigns to tackle the root causes of poverty. It aims to challenge and change the policies of governments and businesses that cause poverty in the developing world. Its network of individuals, groups and professional campaigners has been an integral part of the battle to ensure a fairer deal for the world's poor. If there isn't a local group in your area, WDM can help you to set one up.

Tel: 020 7737 6215
www.wdm.org.uk

Development organizations raise awareness about poor countries, campaign for trade justice, promote development work and, in general, wage war against poverty – 'the only war worth fighting', according to War on Want. For an extensive list see www.oneworld.net/partners

ActionAid
Tel: 020 7561 7561
www.actionaid.org.uk

Did you know...?

The World Social Forum is an annual gathering of people actively resisting the corporate model of globalization and campaigning for justice. It has grown from an attendance of around **25,000** in **2001** in Porto Alegre, Brazil, to the more than **100,000** who gathered in Mumbai, India, in **2004.**

Cafod
Romero Close
Stockwell Road
London SW9 9TY
Tel: 020 7733 7900
www.cafod.org.uk

Christian Aid
35 Lower Marsh
Waterloo
London
SE1 7RL
Tel: 020 7620 4444
www.christian-aid.org.uk

Oxfam
274 Banbury Rd
Oxford OX2 7DZ
Tel: 0870 333 2700
www.oxfam.org.uk

Save the Children
1 St. John's Lane
London
EC1M 4AR
Tel: 020 7012 6400
www.savethechildren.org.uk

War on Want
Fenner Brockway House
37-39 Great Guildford Street
London
SE1 OES
Tel: 020 7620 1111
www.waronwant.org

Virtually protesting

A couple of websites provide interesting reading and will help to keep you on your protest toes.

Globalise Resistance campaigns against the growth of corporate power.

Tel: 020 7053 2071
www.resist.org.uk

Protest Net lists forthcoming demonstrations across the world by city and by issue (eg human rights, animal rights). So you can plan your holidays accordingly. It also has an 'activists' handbook', which has useful advice on how to start a movement, publish a newsletter, get your message out, etc.

www.protest.net

Volunteer force

Before you decide that volunteering is worthy work best left to other people, you should know that things aren't what they used to be. Volunteering has had a facelift – it's now trendy, gets a good press, and millions of people nationwide are doing it.

It's no longer just about photocopying, stuffing envelopes or rattling a tin can in the high street. It's much more about passing on and acquiring skills, and it's a lot more interesting than it used to be. You can search out the right slot for you to help people in your community, across the country or abroad. And with the advent of modern technology, you can even volunteer to work on some projects without leaving home.

The National Centre for Volunteering says about 22 million people in Britain volunteer annually, and that the economic value of the sector is more than £45 billion.

Whatever your age, ethnic background or skills, you can contribute. Your commitment can be flexible: it could be a one-off, a couple of hours a week or long term. Choose to volunteer locally or with a national campaign. And you can get out of it as much as you give – maybe more.

TimeBank and Do-it make volunteering easy. You register your details and interests, and are matched up with suitable voluntary work on offer. Bit like a dating agency.

TimeBank
Tel: 0845 601 4008
www.timebank.org.uk

Do-it
Tel: 020 7925 2530
www.do-it.org.uk

See also:

Community Service Volunteers
Tel: 020 7239 9556
www.csv.org.uk

The National Centre for Volunteering
Tel: 020 7520-8900
www.volunteering.org.uk

For the over-50s:

Experience Corps
Tel: 0800 106080
www.experiencecorps.co.uk

Retired and Senior Volunteer Programme
Tel: 020 7643 1385
www.csv-rsvp.org.uk

United Nations Volunteers runs an online network where 'net volunteers' from across the world help organizations in developing countries. They design websites, translate, do research, write articles, give legal advice, etc.

www.onlinevolunteering.org

Voluntary Service Overseas seeks volunteers with professional qualifications and experience for work abroad, mainly in Africa and Asia. Most jobs – in health, education, etc – require a two-year commitment, but VSO has a scheme whereby employees of partner companies can do a 6- to 12-month stint.

Tel: 020 8780 7500
www.vso.org.uk

Community spirit

The best way to ensure that your local community thrives is to participate in and engage with it in any way you can. Communities need local heroes: people who are willing to give time and energy to make local life better.

You can start by volunteering (see above), or if you feel that there's something that needs to be done but nobody's doing it, you could make it happen. It could be to do with crime prevention, cycling, recycling, looking after public spaces, etc. If you want to start up your own group, contact your local **Council for Voluntary Services**.

Tel: 0114 278 6636
www.nacvs.org.uk

The **National Federation of Community Organizations** has lots of relevant information and publishes a useful guide: *Community Start Up*.

Tel: 020 7387 7887
www.communitymatters.org.uk

The **Community Development Foundation** is also a good source of information and has a guide to community action and sustainable development, called *A Better Place To Live*.

www.cdf.org.uk

You could also do good for your community by becoming a local councillor or a school governor.

Listen up

'You must be the change you want to see in the world'

Mohandas K Gandhi (1869-1948),
Indian nationalist leader

Don't forget about backing local shops and restaurants by giving them your custom and avoiding the chain gangs like McDonalds and Starbucks (see *Consuming Passions* chapter). Encourage people to buy locally and try to promote trade among local businesses.

LETS (Local Exchange Trading System) is a scheme under which people exchange goods and services without recourse to money. It's open to people of all ages and skills, and helps forge links within a community. There are more than 450 schemes operating in Britain, involving tens of thousands of people. Using LETS is like ring-fencing your money so that it stays within the community.

Letslink UK tells you about your nearest local LETS. It also gives advice and support if you want to set up a scheme in your area.

Tel: 020 7607 7852
www.letslinkuk.net

Lets Scotland
Tel: 01309 676128
www.letslinkscotland.org.uk

Donor card sharp

Organ transplant operations save lives, and you can make sure they save even more by indicating your readiness to be an organ donor in the event of your death. Hundreds of people die each year waiting for transplants of kidneys, hearts, lungs and liver. Every year there are more than 5,000 people awaiting operations, but fewer than 3,000 are carried out because of a shortage of organs. The NHS UK Transplant website tells how to become a donor. You need to register, and then to carry a donor card. So become a card-carrying member of the public and put yourself on the books to make a life-saving gift – more than 11 million people have already done so. And make sure you tell family members about your decision.

NHS UK Transplant
Tel: 0845 6060400
www.uktransplant.org.uk

Job satisfaction

Once you've done a stretch as a volunteer, you could be ripe for a job in the charity sector. Or you may have skills acquired elsewhere that you now want to put at the service of charities and not-for-profit groups. The organizations below will point you in the right direction.

Subscribe to **People & Planet's Ethical Careers Service** and you get three issues of *Your Future* magazine plus jobs available sent to your inbox.

Tel: 01865 245678
www.ethicalcareers.org

Green Work has jobs in the environmental sector.

Tel: 0870 787 5587
www.greenwork.co.uk

In solidarity

If you want to get mad at Mugabe, support Suu Kyi, look lively for Lula or be *semper fidelis* to Cuba, there's a group you can sign up with.

Asia

Afghanistan
Revolutionary Association of the Women of Afghanistan
Tel: 01453 766456
www.rawa.org

Burma
The Burma Campaign UK
020 7324 4710
www.burmacampaign.org.uk

Indonesia
Tapol – The Indonesian Human Rights Campaign
Tel: 020 8771 2904
www.tapol.org

Palestine
Palestine Solidarity Campaign
Tel: 020 7700 6192
www.palestinecampaign.org

South Asia
South Asia Solidarity Group
Tel: 020 7267 0923
www.southasiasolidarity.org

Awaaz -South Asia Watch
www.awaazsaw.org

Tibet
Free Tibet Campaign
Tel: 020 7833 9958
www.freetibet.org

West Papua
West Papua Association UK
Tel: 020 7265 9307
www.westpapua.org/wpauk.html

Oxford Papuan Rights Campaign
www.westpapua.org

Africa

Akina Mama wa Africa
(solidarity among African
women)
Tel: 020 7713 5166
www.akinamama.org

Justice Africa
Tel: 020 78377888
www.justiceafrica.org

Angola/Mozambique
**Mozambique Angola
Committee**
Tel: 020 7387 0921

South Africa
Action for Southern Africa
Tel: 020 7833 3133
www.actsa.org

Western Sahara
Western Sahara Campaign
Tel: 0845 458 2953
wsc.members.gn.apc.org

Zimbabwe
Zimbabwe Vigil Coalition
www.zimvigil.co.uk

Latin America

Argentina
**Argentine Solidarity
Campaign**
www.geocities.com/argentinesc

Brazil
Brazil Network
Tel: 020 7732 8810
www.brazilnetwork.org.uk

Central American
**Central America Women's
Network**
Tel: 020 7833 4075
www.cawn.org

Colombia
**Colombia Solidarity
Campaign**
Tel: 07743 743041
www.colombiasolidarity.org.uk

Justice for Colombia
www.justiceforcolombia.org

Cuba
Cuba Solidarity Campaign
0207 263-6452
www.cuba-solidarity.org.uk

El Salvador Network
Tel: 0151 7287118
www.esnet.co.uk

Guatemala
Guatemala Solidarity Network
www.guatemalasolidarity.org.uk

Haiti
Haiti Support Group
0208 525 0456
www.haitisupport.gn.apc.org

Mexico
Edinburgh-Chiapas Solidarity Group
Tel: 0131 5576242
www.edinchiapas.org.uk

Nicaragua
Nicaragua Solidarity Campaign
Tel: 020 7272 9619
www.nicaraguasc.org.uk

Peru
Peru Support Group
Tel: 020 7354 9825
www.perusupportgroup.co.uk

Easy does it

Contact your MP about an issue that has raised your concern

Join a campaigning group

Try volunteering for something (you might like it!)

ABOUT THE NEW INTERNATIONALIST

www.newint.org

New Internationalist Publications is a co-operative with offices in Oxford (England), Adelaide (Australia), Toronto (Canada) and Christchurch (New Zealand/Aotearoa). It exists to report on the issues of world poverty and inequality; to focus attention on the unjust relationship between the powerful and powerless in both rich and poor nations; to debate and campaign for the radical changes necessary within and between those nations if the basic material and spiritual needs of all are to be met; and to bring to life the people, the ideas, the action in the fight for global justice.

The monthly *New Internationalist* magazine now has more than 75,000 subscribers worldwide. In addition to the magazine, the co-operative publishes the One World Almanac and the One World

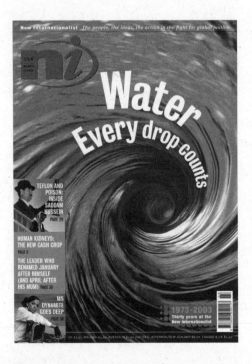

Calendar, both containing an outstanding collection of full-colour photographs. It also publishes books, including: the successful series of No-Nonsense Guides to the key issues in the world today; cookbooks containing recipes and cultural information from around the world; and photographic books on topics such as Nomadic Peoples and Water. The NI is the English-language publisher of the biennial reference book The World Guide, written by the Instituto del Tercer Mundo in Uruguay.

The co-operative is financially independent but aims to break even; any surpluses are reinvested so as to bring New Internationalist publications to as many people as possible.

'The *New Internationalist* is independent, lively and properly provocative, helping keep abreast of important developments in parts of our globe that risk marginalization. Read it!'
      ARCHBISHOP DESMOND TUTU, Cape Town, South Africa

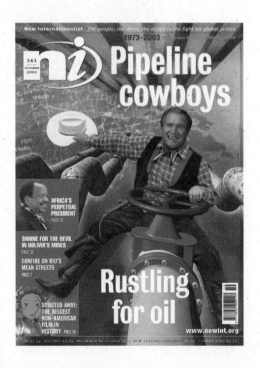

A No-Nonsense view of the world

"The most accessible and enjoyable means for people with hurried lives to find out how the world really works."
George Monbiot, environmentalist, campaigner, and author

The No-Nonsense series provides a clear overview of issues facing today's world. Titles include:

The No-Nonsense Guide to....
- Water **new!**
- Women's Rights **new!**
- Global Media **new!**
- Islam **new!**
- World Poverty
- Terrorism
- Indigenous Peoples
- HIV/AIDS
- International Development
- International Migration
- Democracy
- Globalization
- The Arms Trade
- Class, Caste & Hierarchies
- World History
- Sexual Diversity
- Climate Change
- Fair Trade

"The No-Nonsense Guides target those topics that a large army of voters care about, but that politicos evade."
The Independent

To find out more about the series, or to place an order, visit **www.newint.org/shop** and follow the links to the 'Books' page.

UK credit/debit card order line: **(01709) 513999**